INNER ARTIST COLORING BOOKS

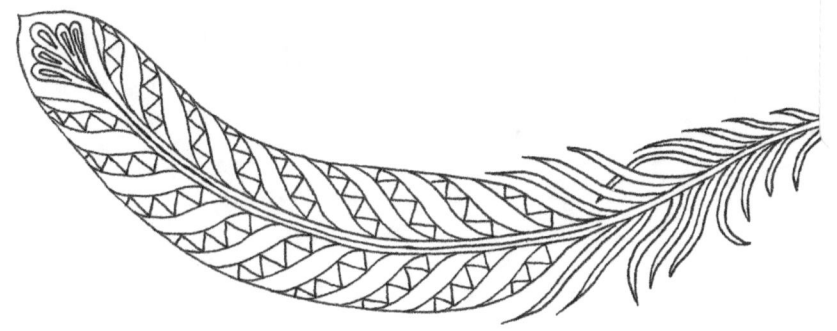

Coloring for Relaxation

- Inspirational Quotes & Words -

By Allison L. Thomson

ISBN-13: 978-1530546268
ISBN-10: 1530546265

inner-artist@outlook.com

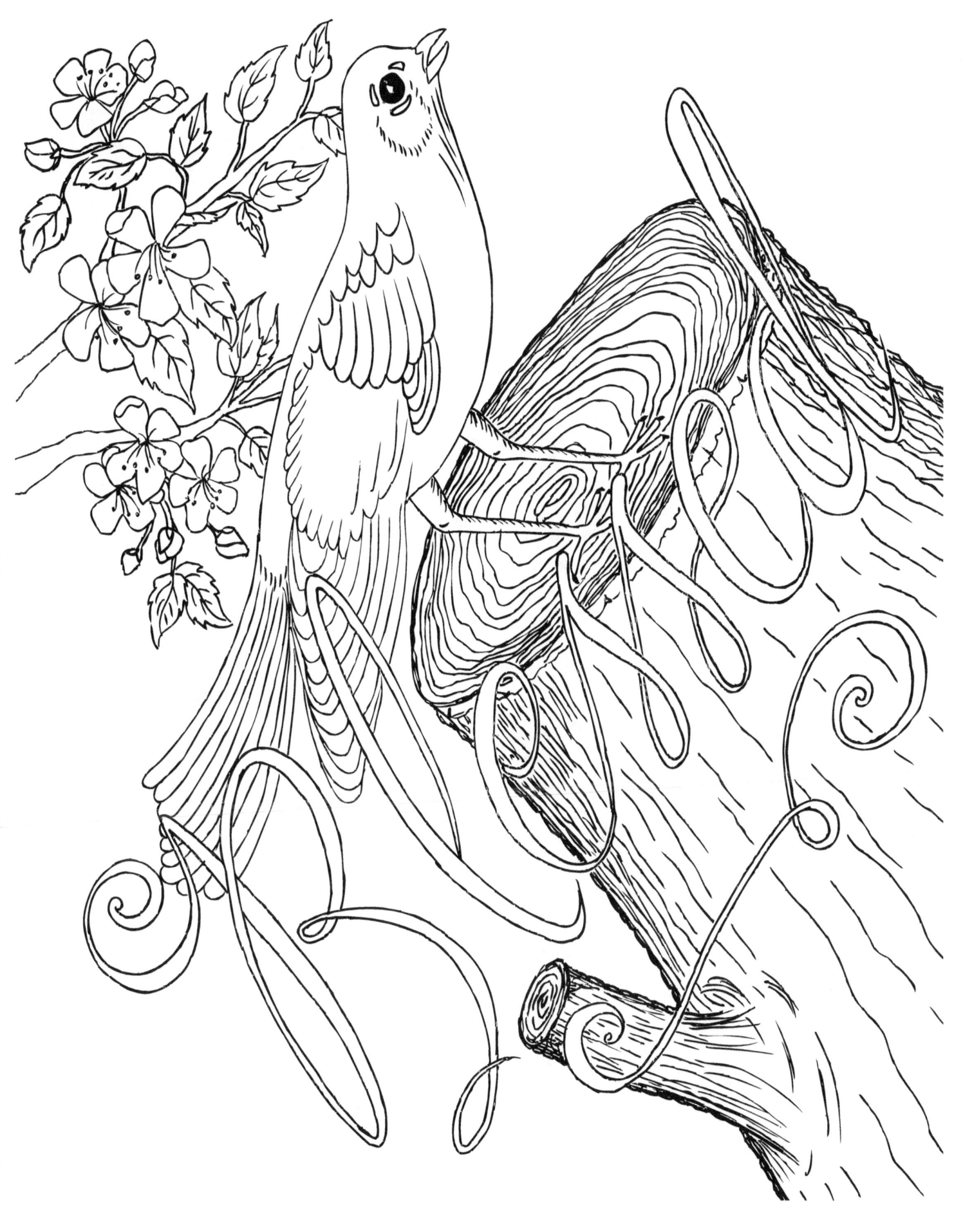

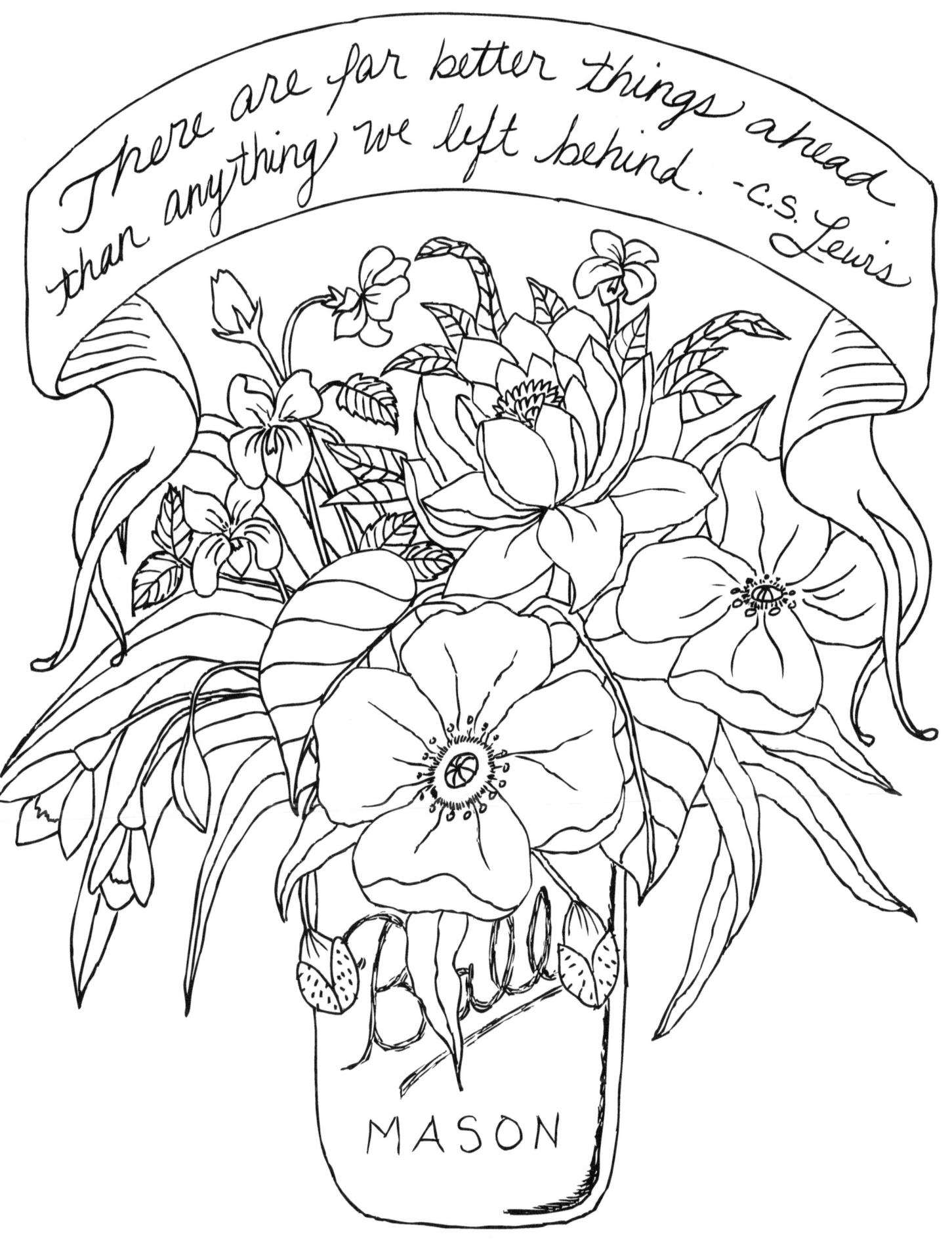

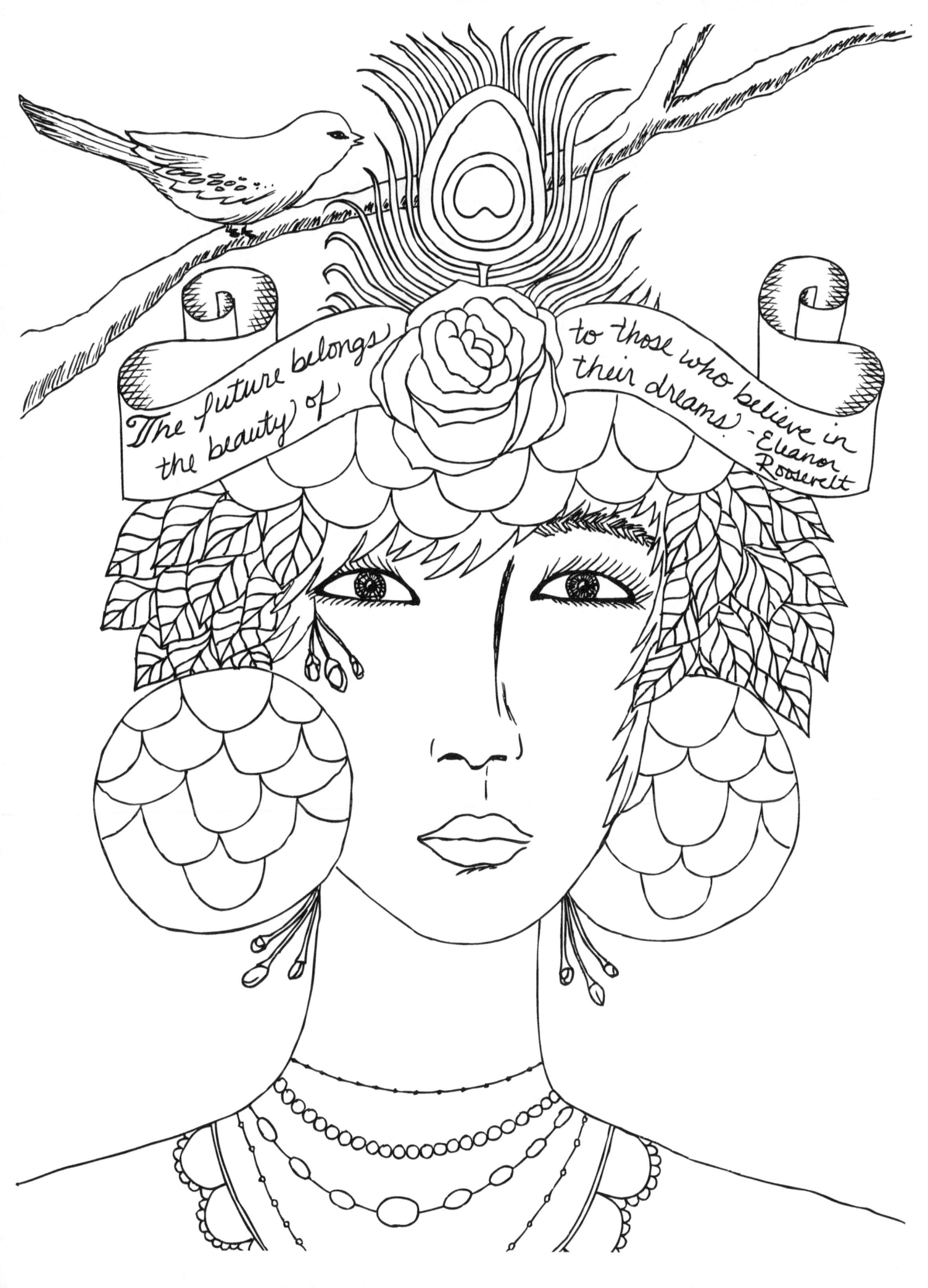

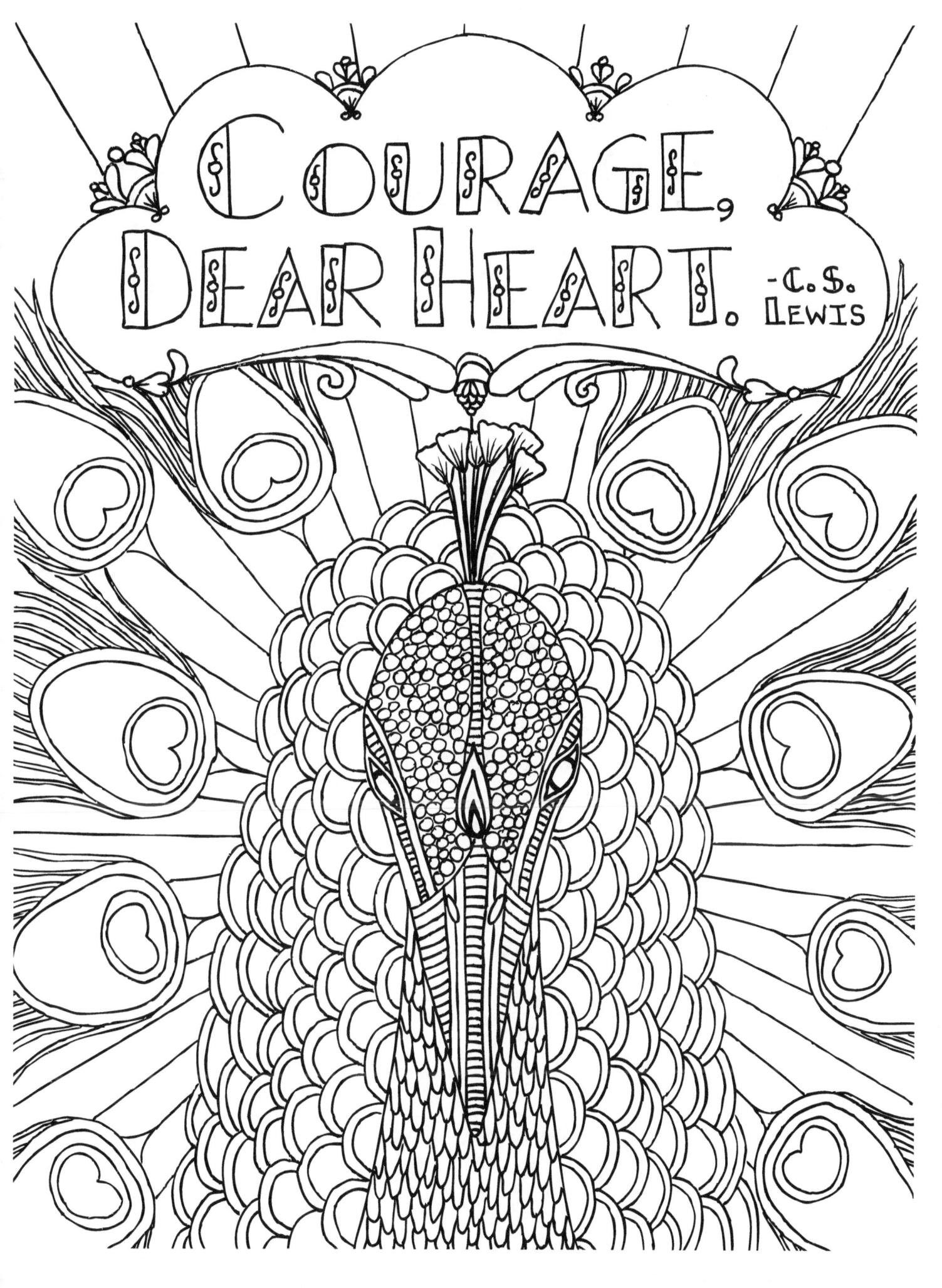

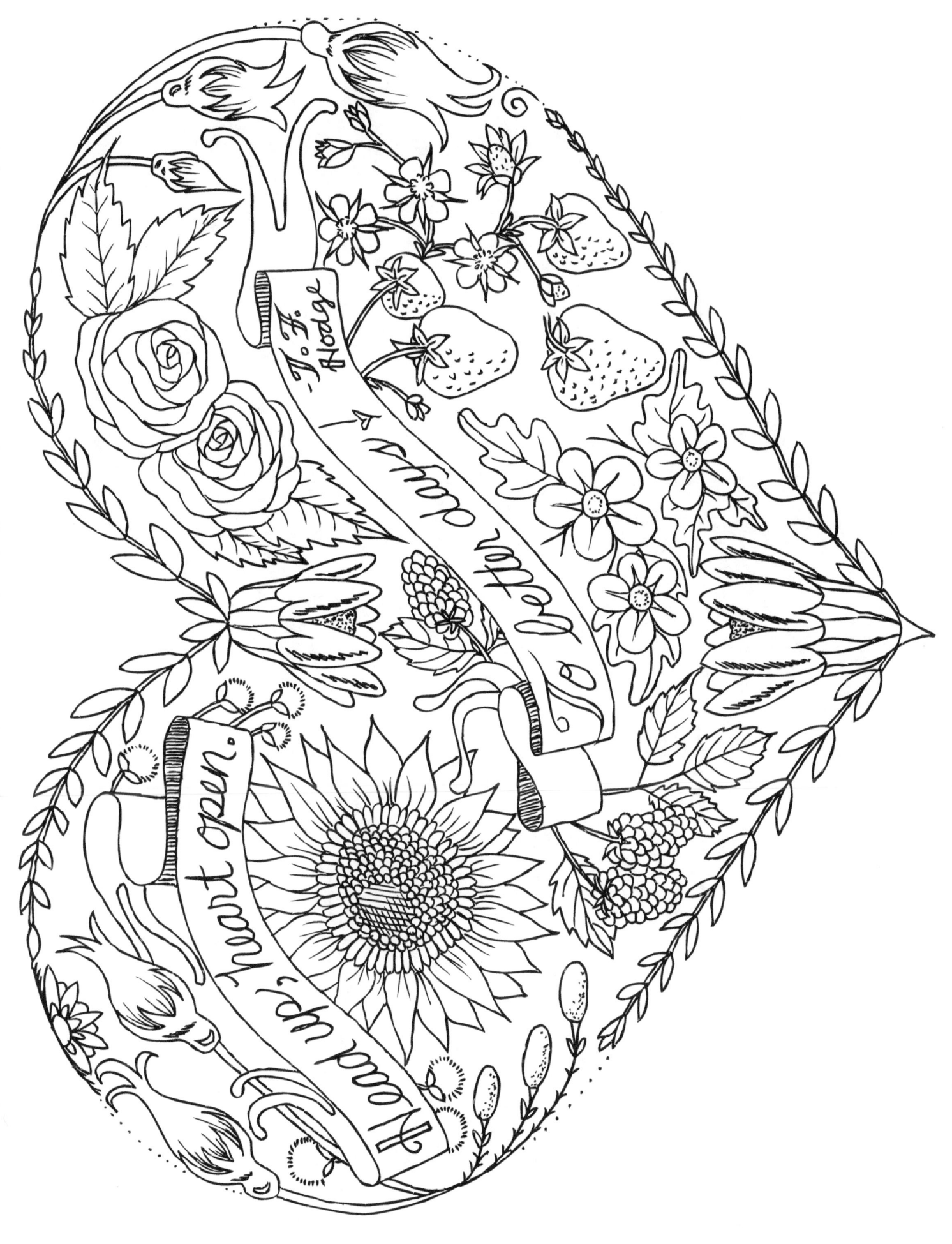

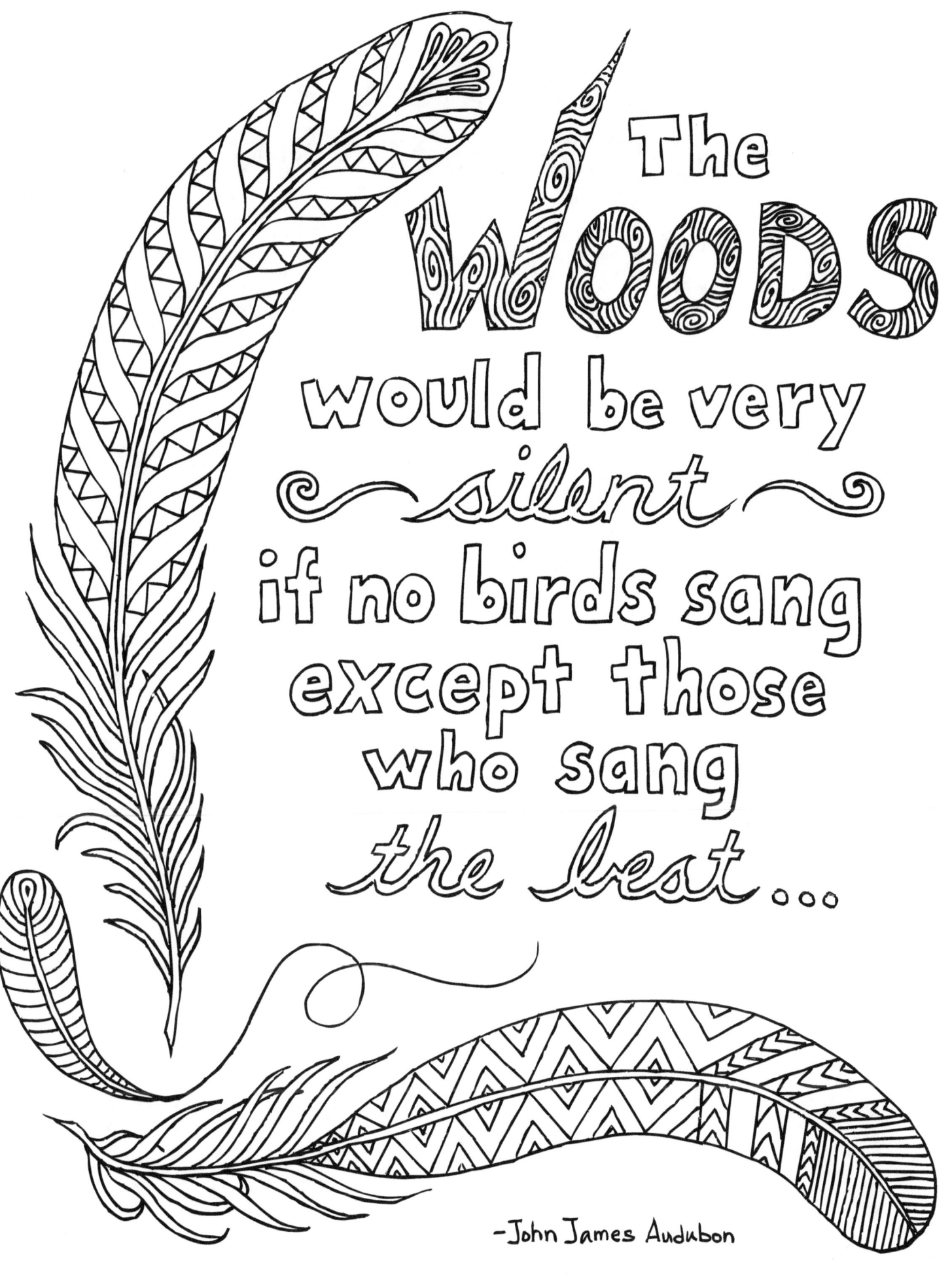

The
WOODS
would be very
~ silent ~
if no birds sang
except those
who sang
the best...

-John James Audubon

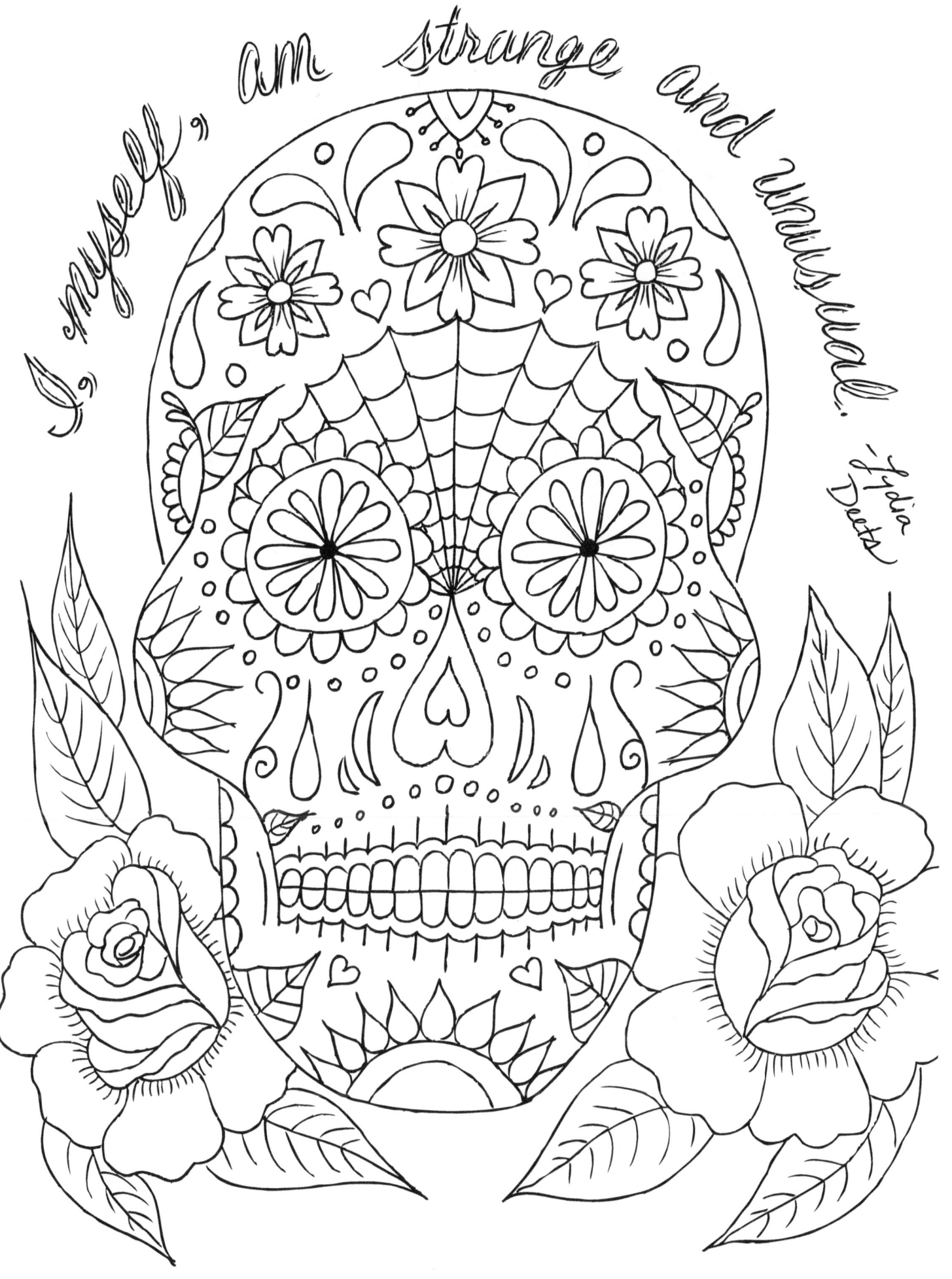

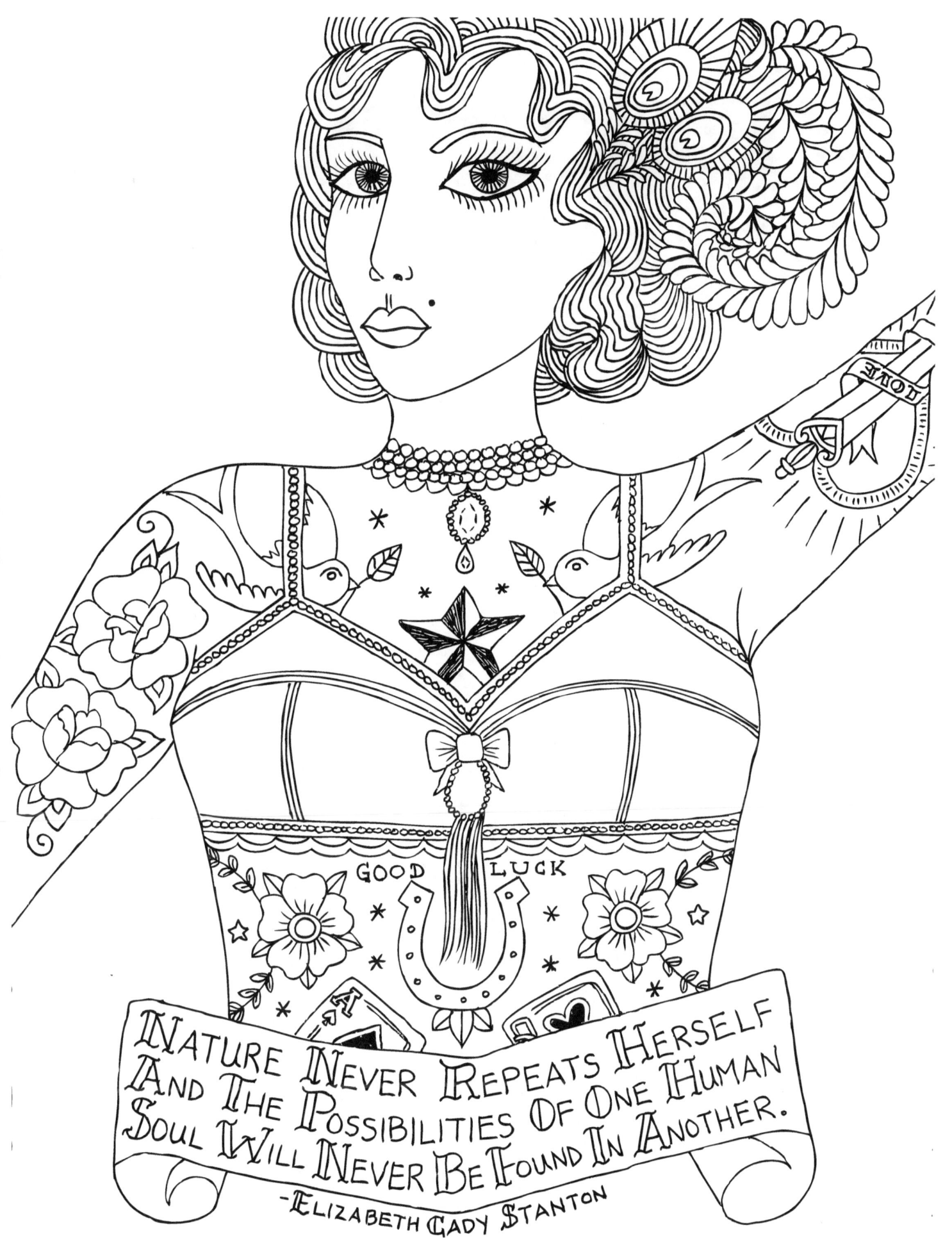

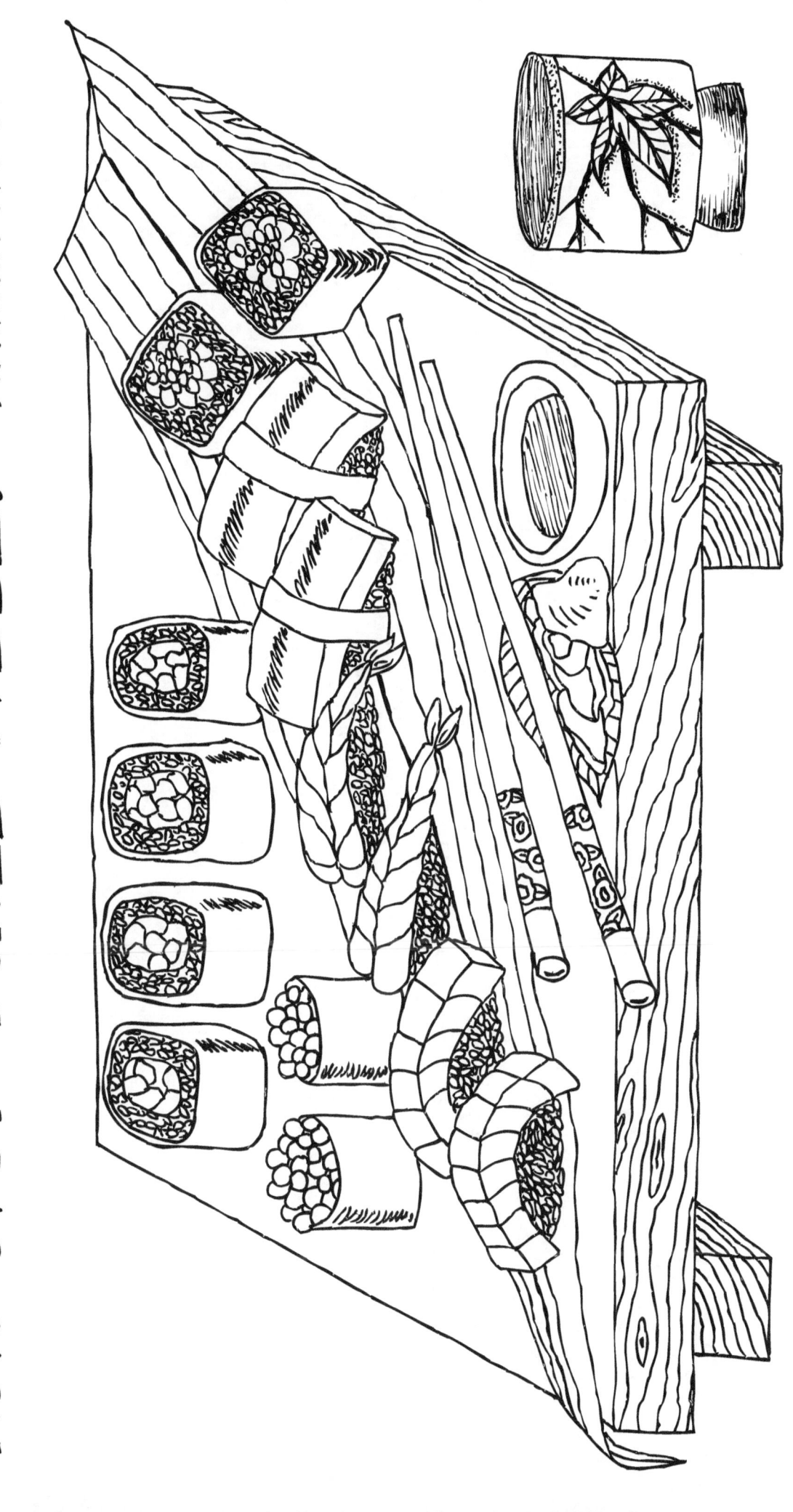

ONE CANNOT THINK WELL, LOVE WELL, SLEEP WELL, IF ONE HAS NOT DINED WELL. —VIRGINIA WOOLF

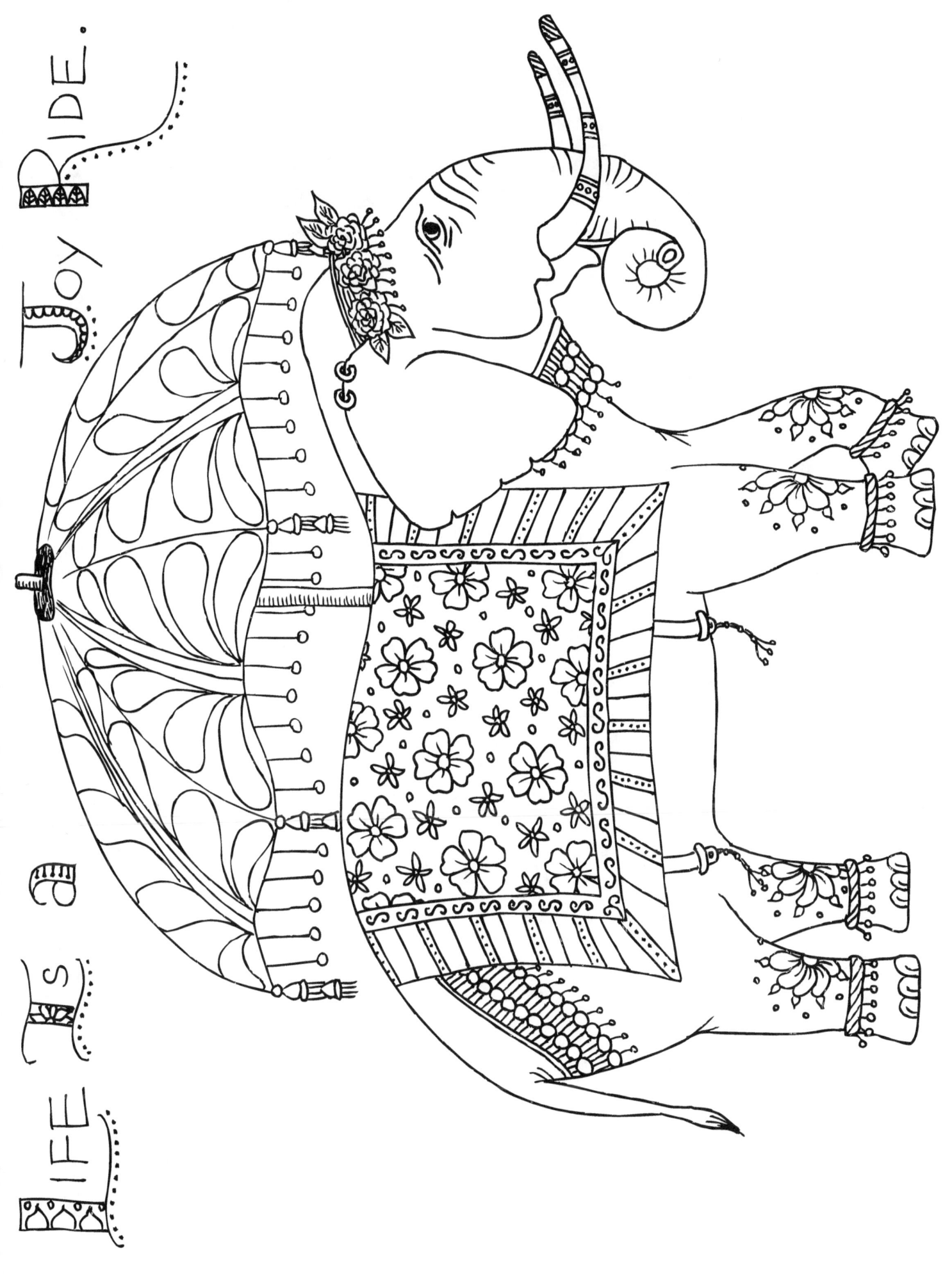

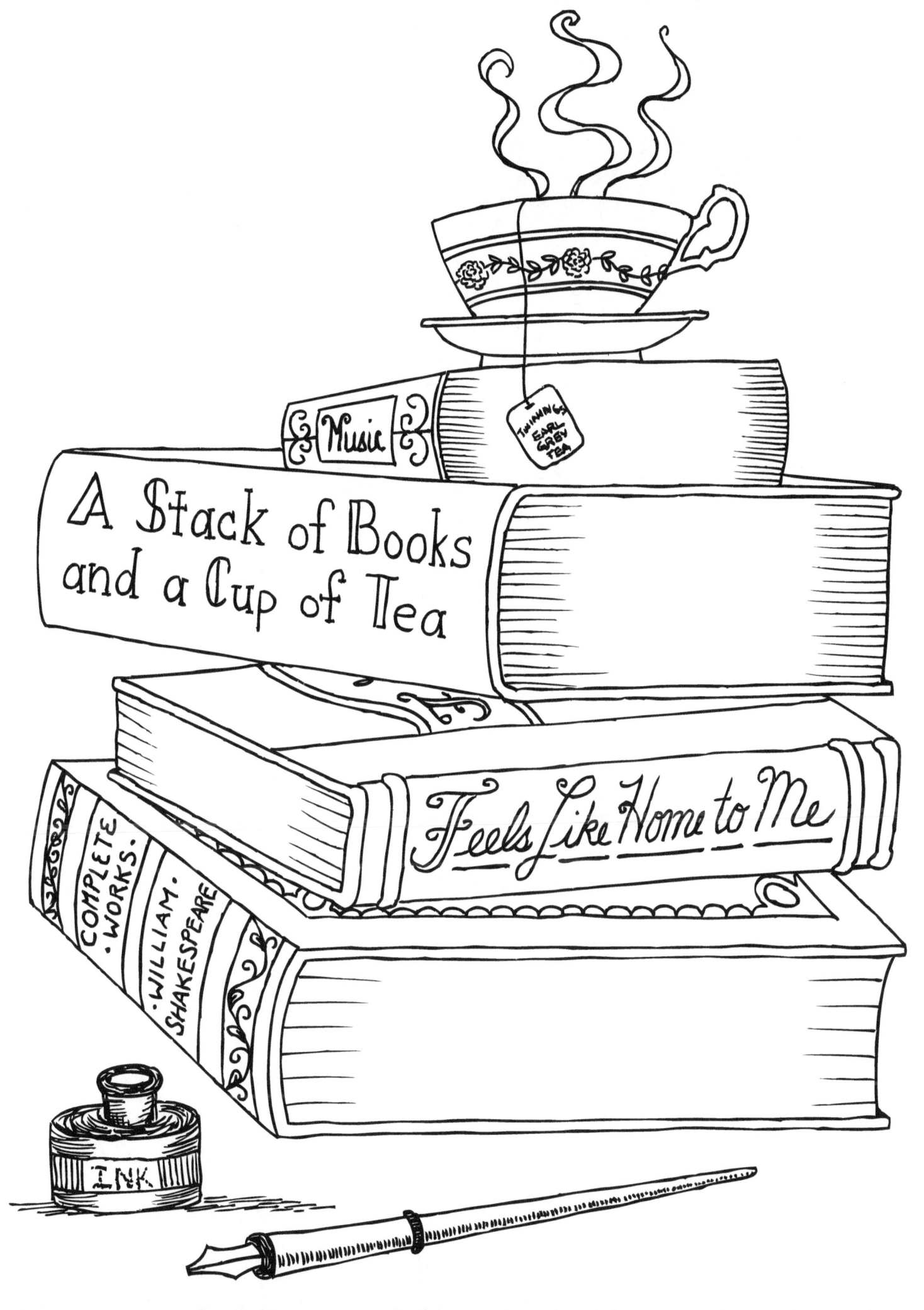

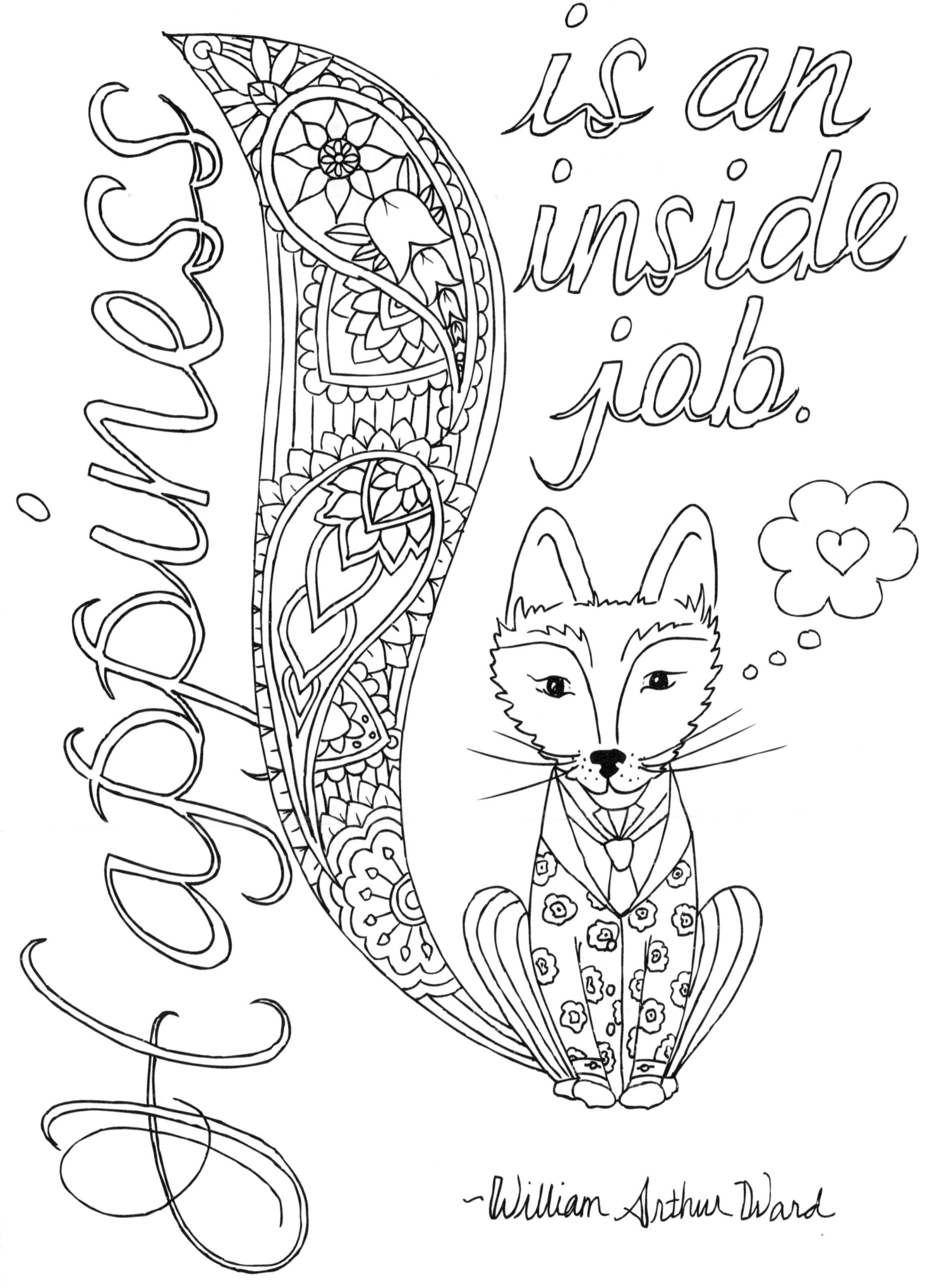

Happiness is an inside job.

-William Arthur Ward

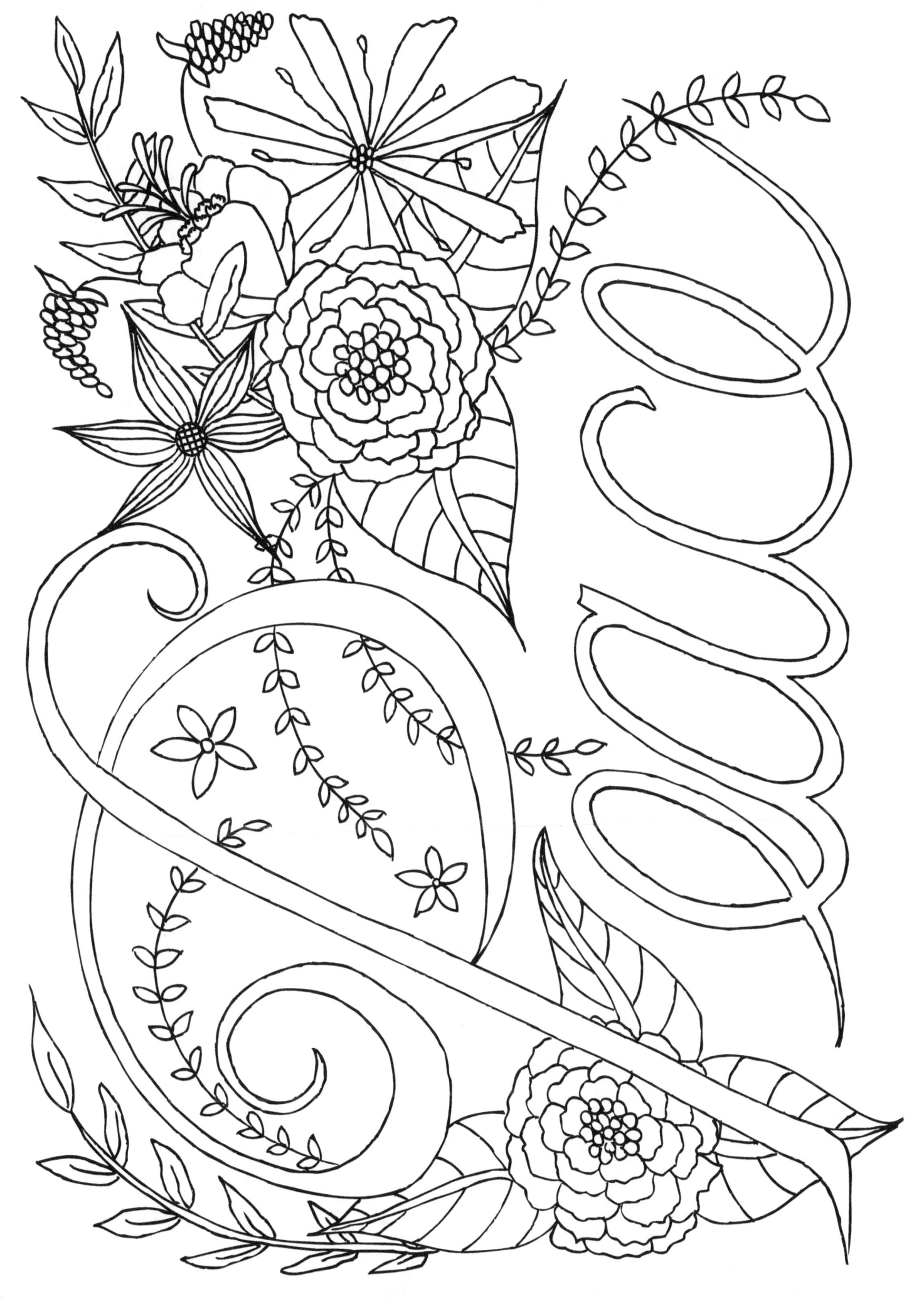

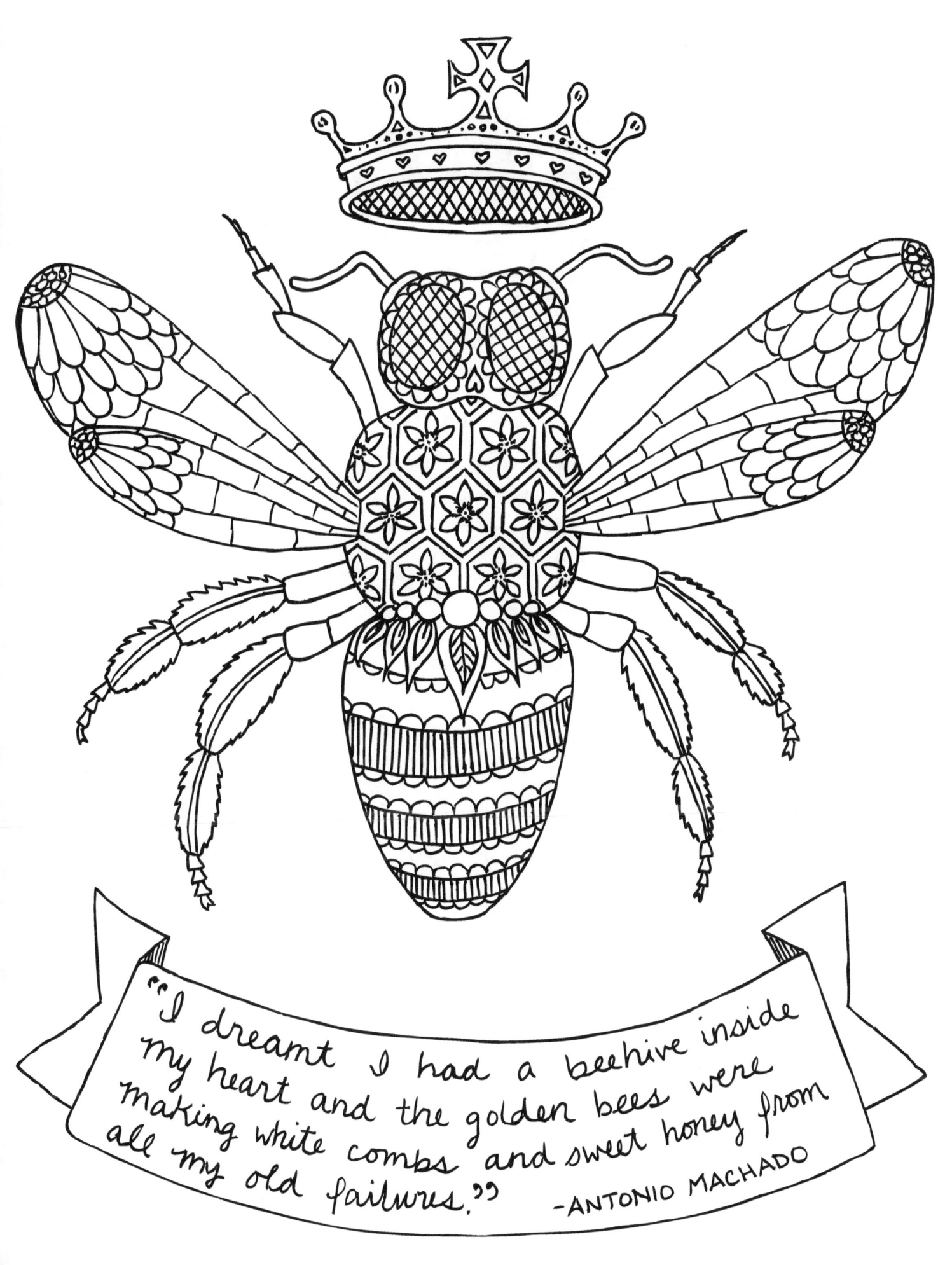

"I dreamt I had a beehive inside my heart and the golden bees were making white combs and sweet honey from all my old failures." -ANTONIO MACHADO

And the day came

when the risk to remain
tight in the bud was more
painful than the risk it took to blossom

- ANIAS NIN

THE EARTH
Laughs
IN FLOWERS

-Ralph Waldo Emerson

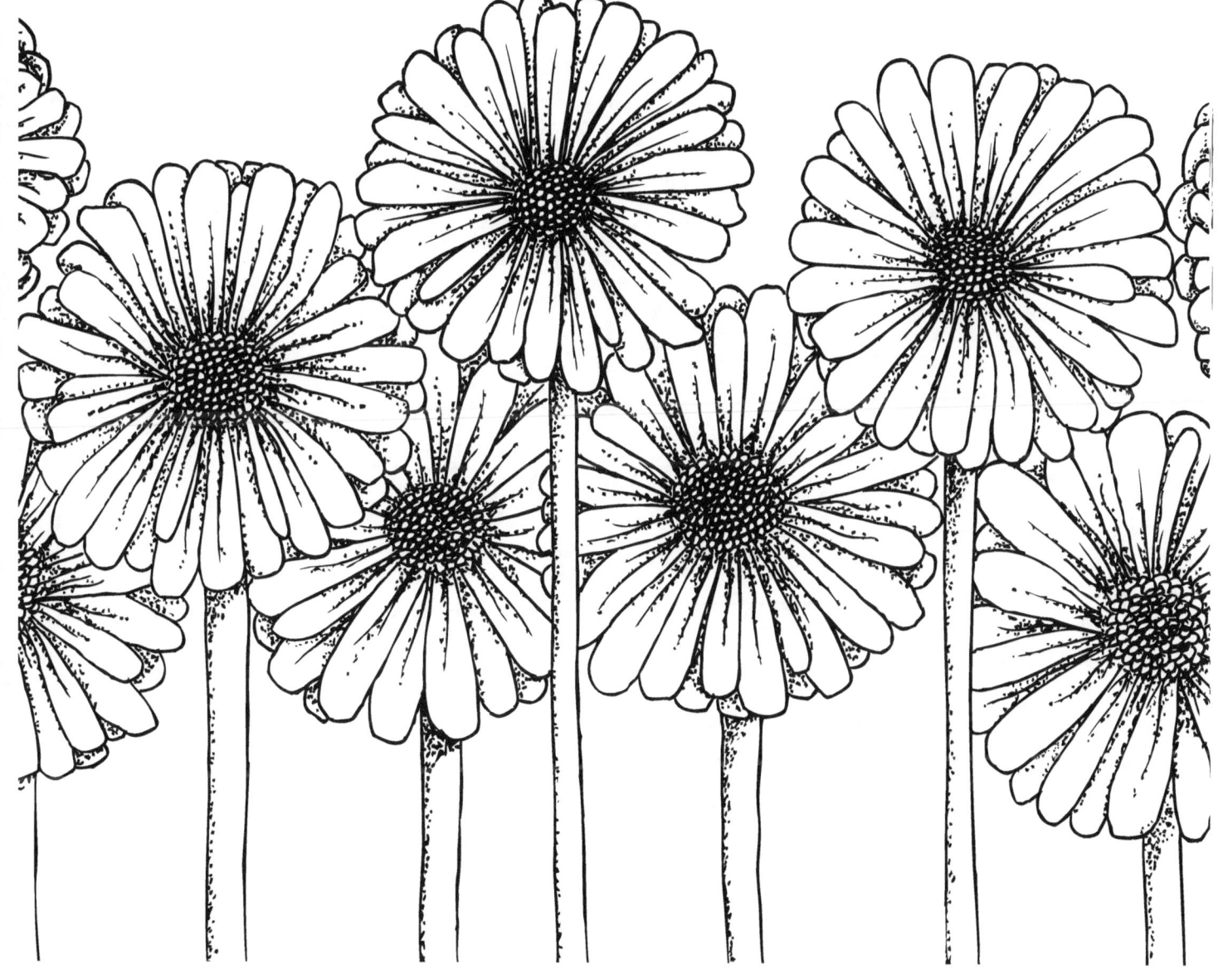

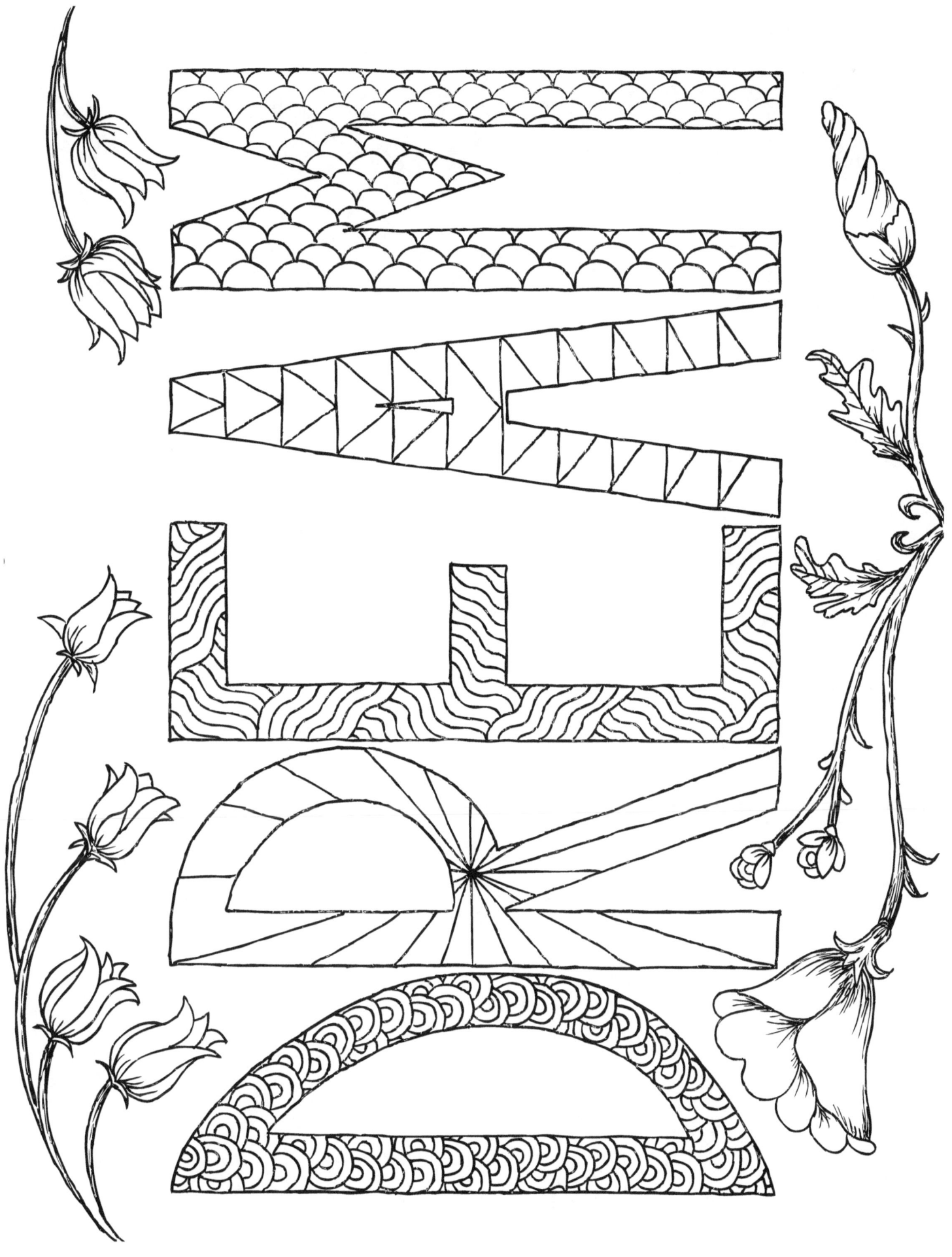

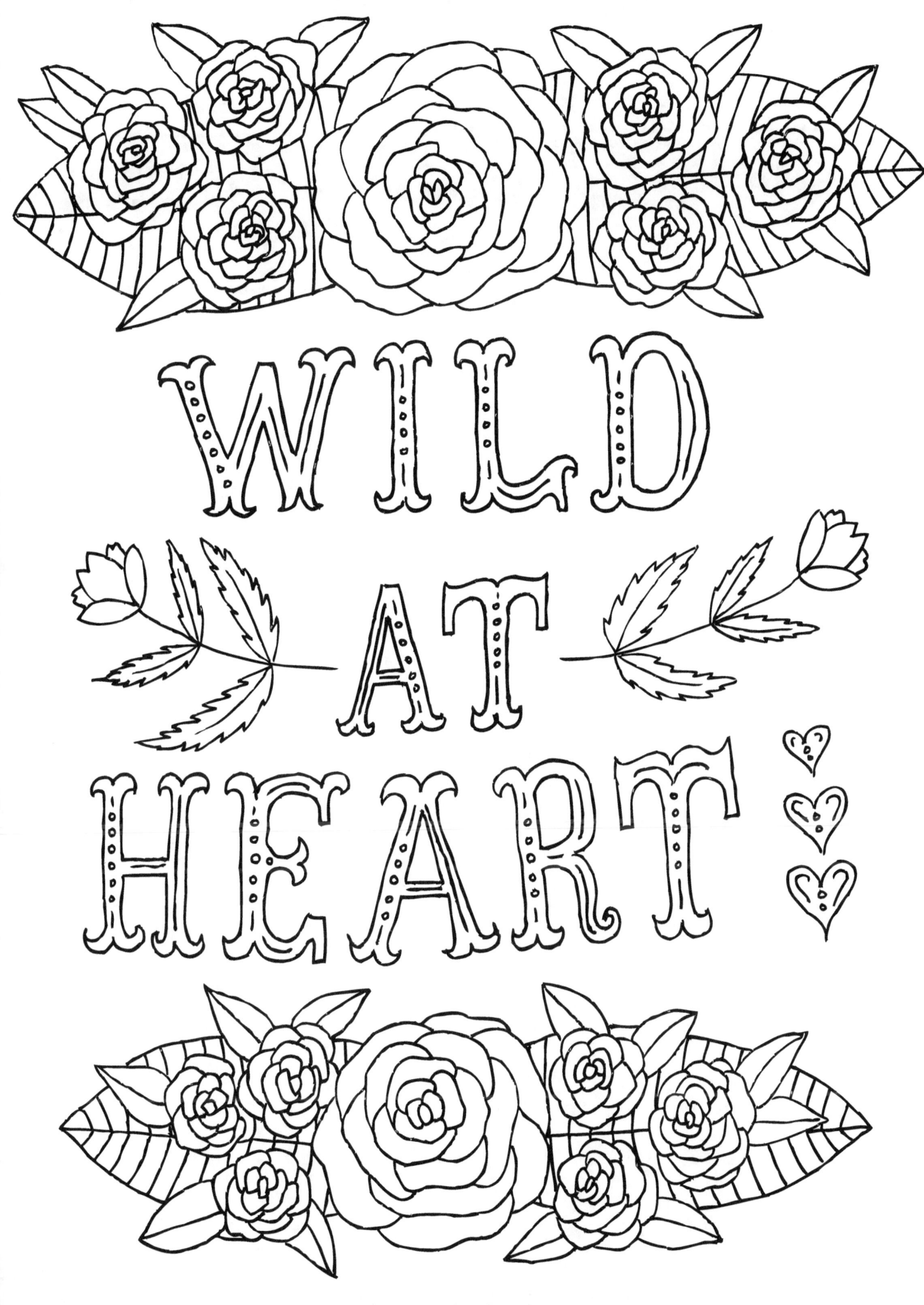

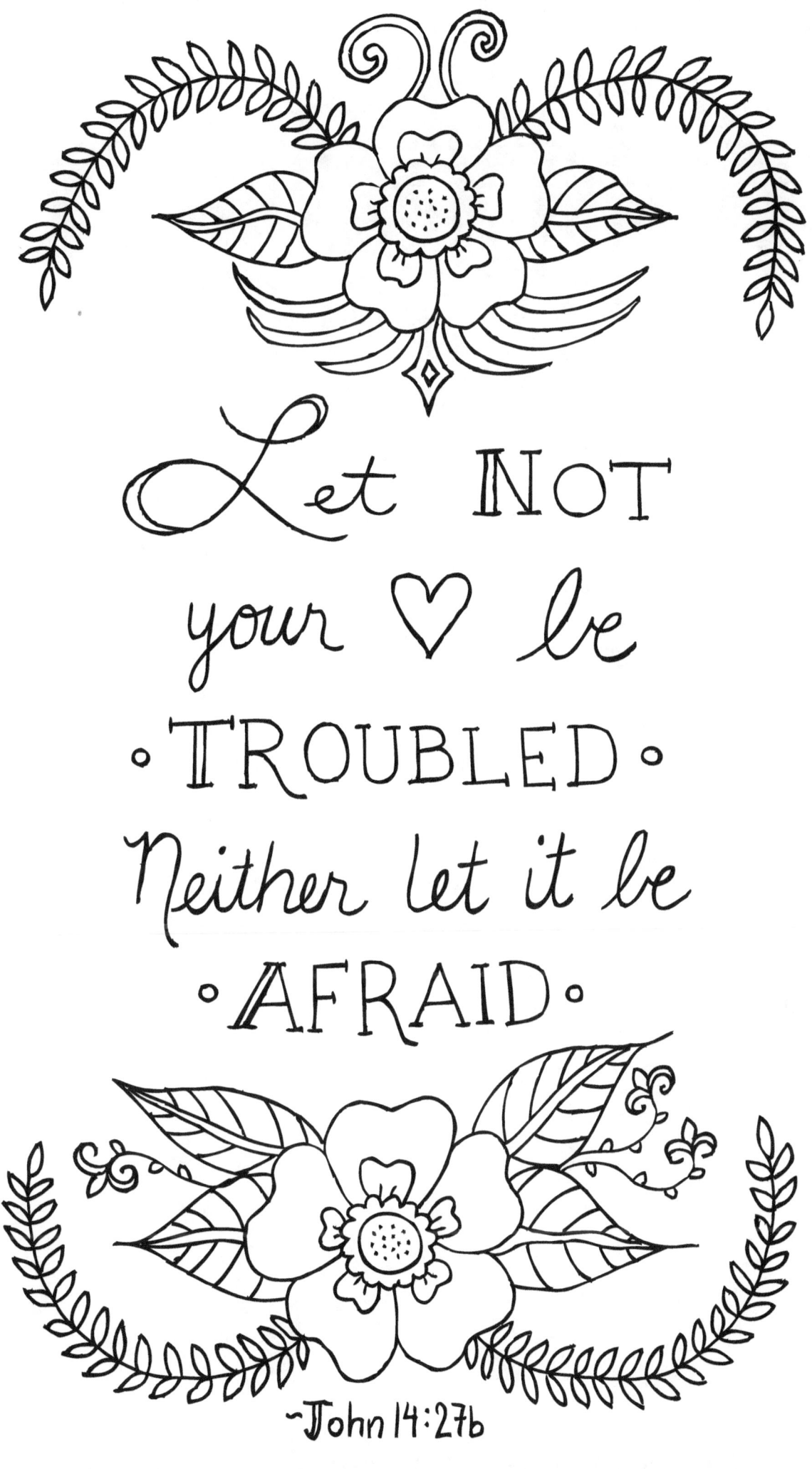

Let Not your ♡ be
• TROUBLED •
Neither let it be
• AFRAID •

~John 14:27b

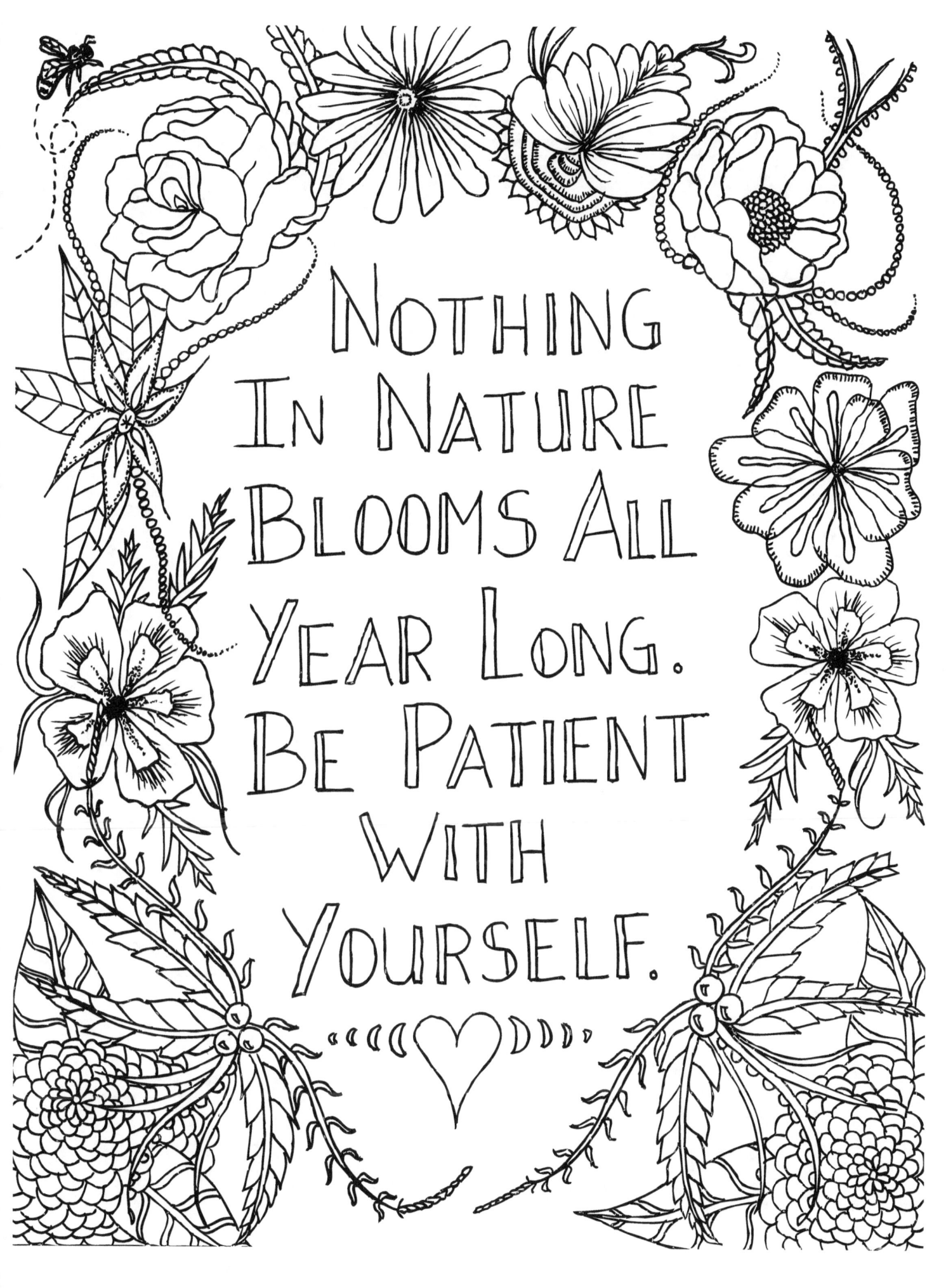

NOTHING IN NATURE BLOOMS ALL YEAR LONG. BE PATIENT WITH YOURSELF.

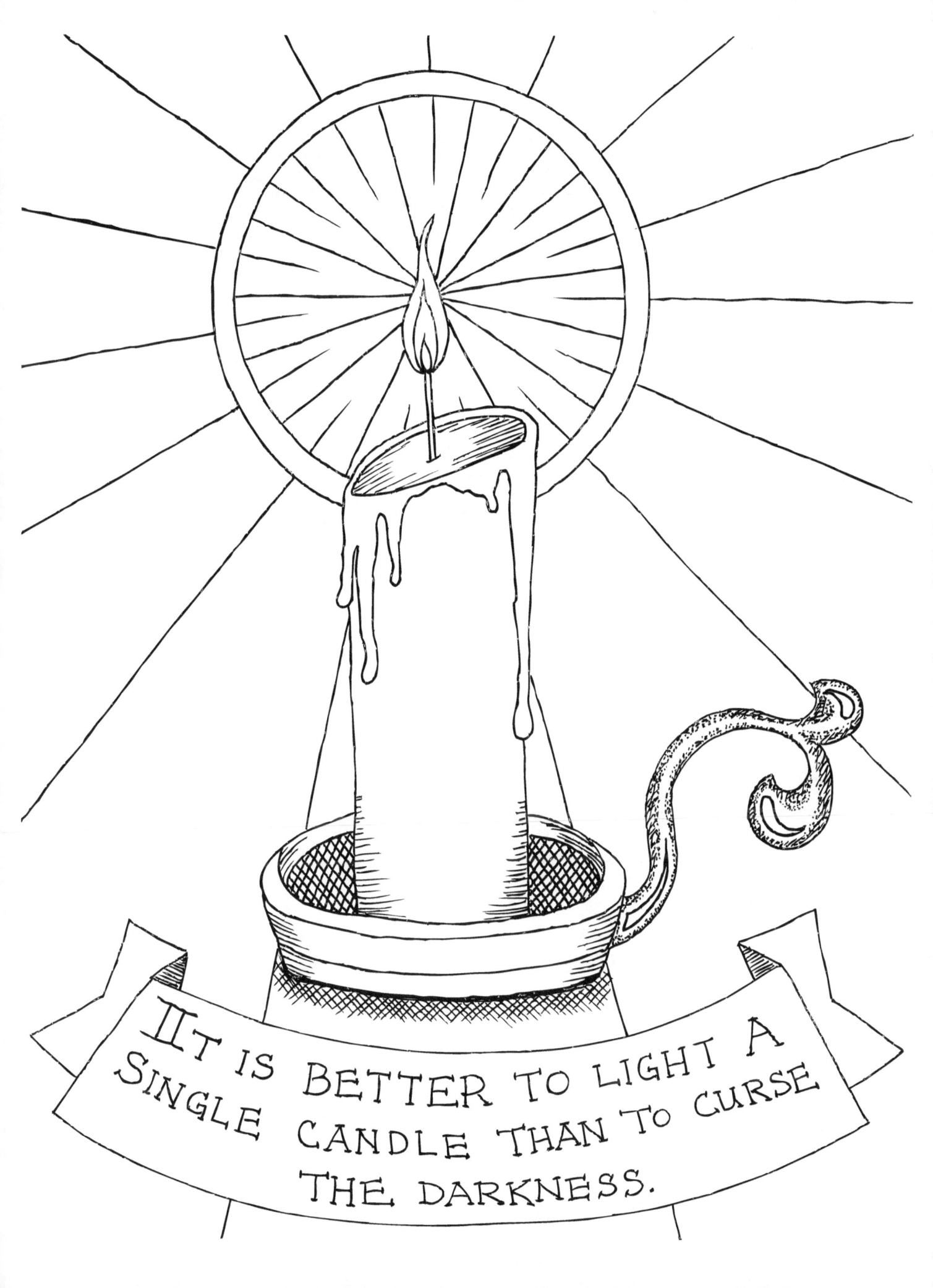

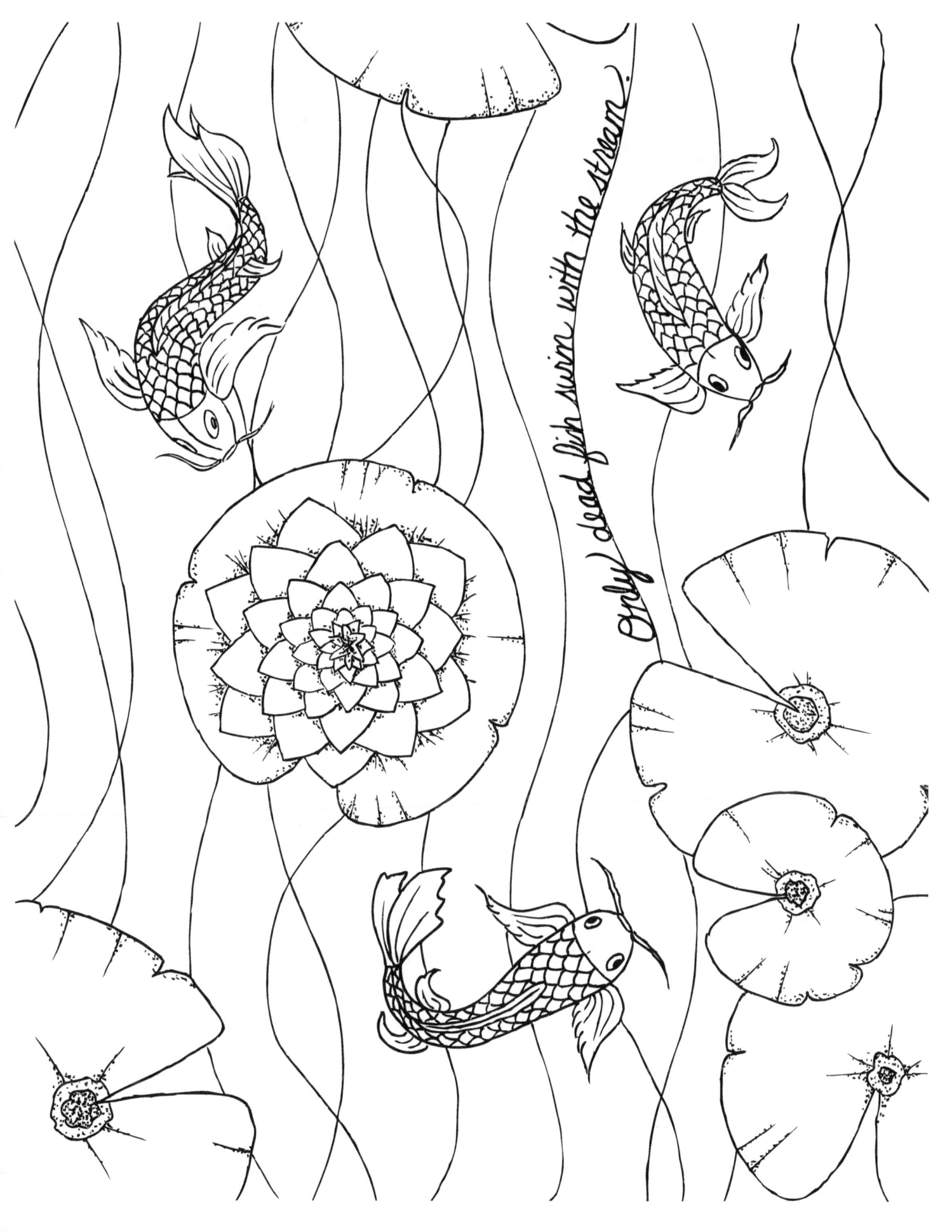

Only dead fish swim with the stream.

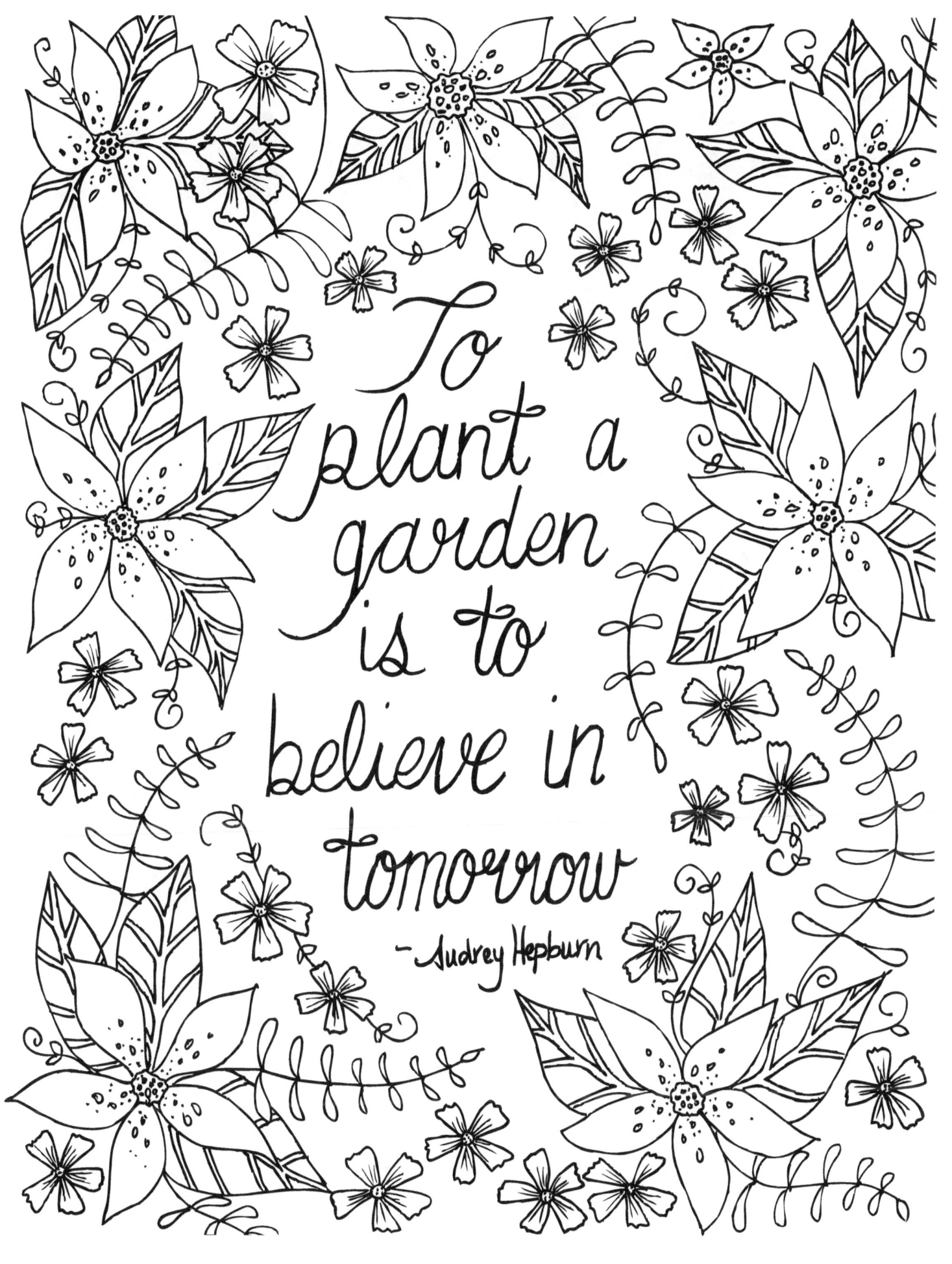

To plant a garden is to believe in tomorrow

— Audrey Hepburn

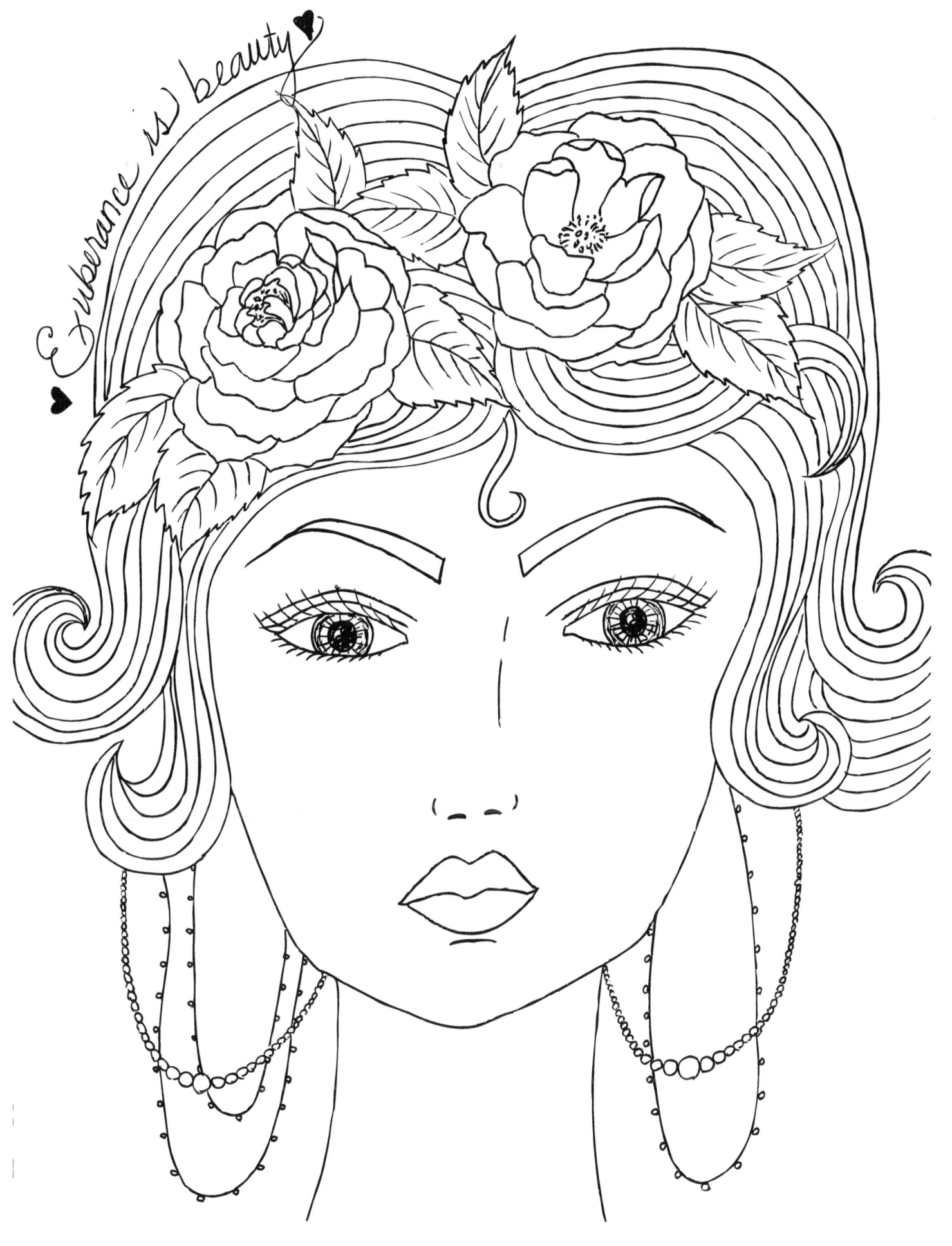

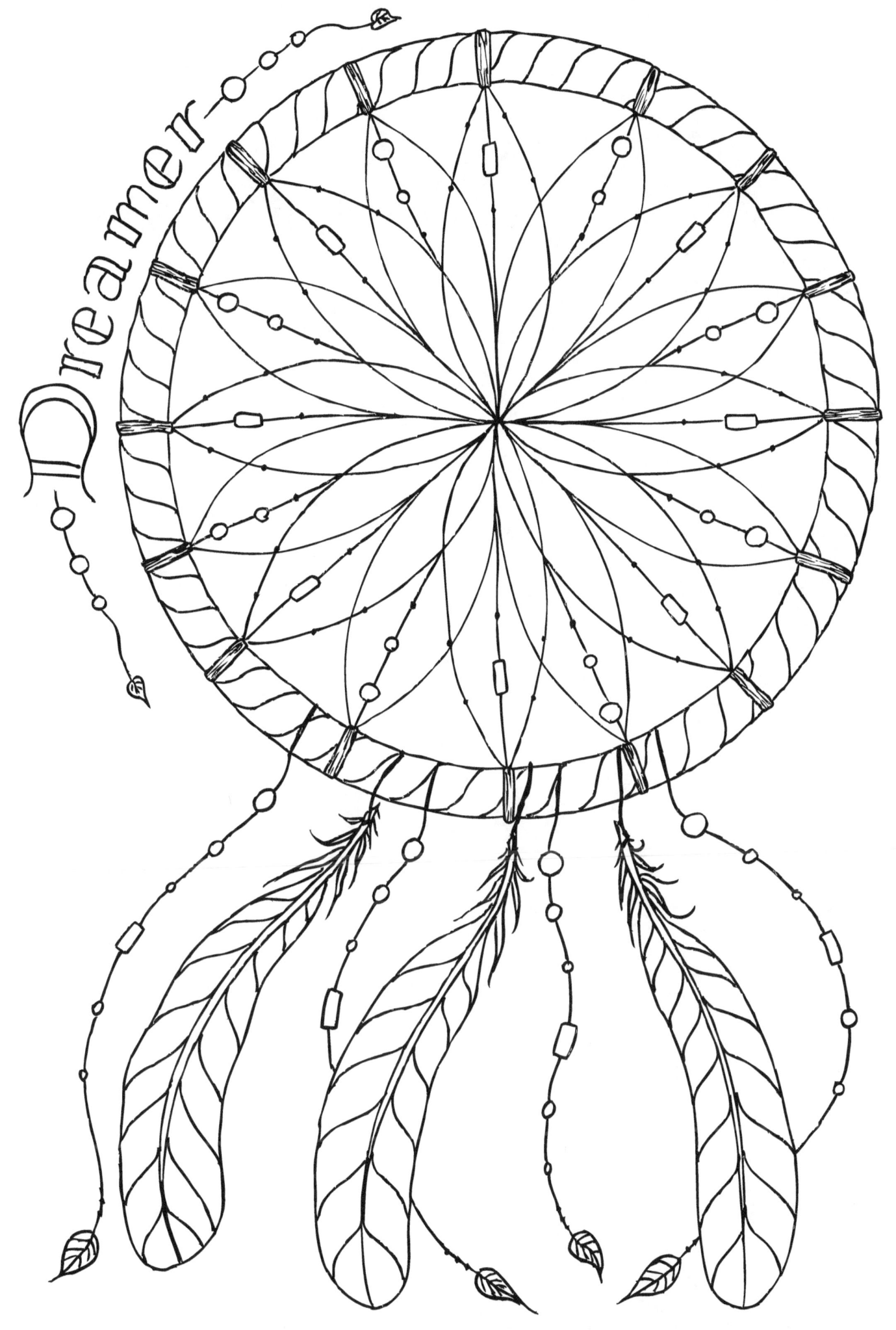

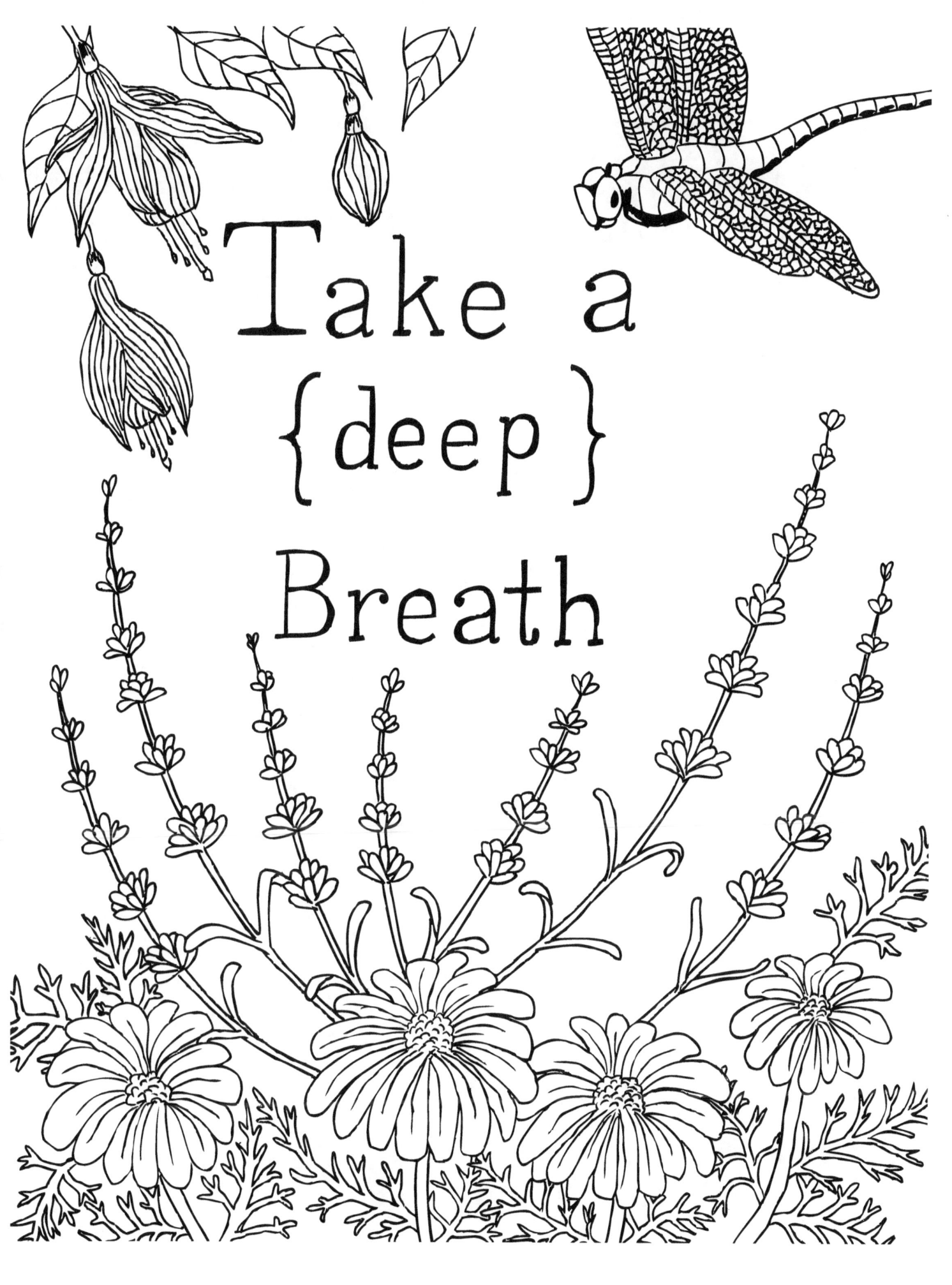

With Mirth & Laughter
Let Old Wrinkles Come.
~ Shakespeare

To lose balance sometimes for LOVE is part of living a balanced life.

-Elizabeth Gilbert (Eat. Pray. Love.)

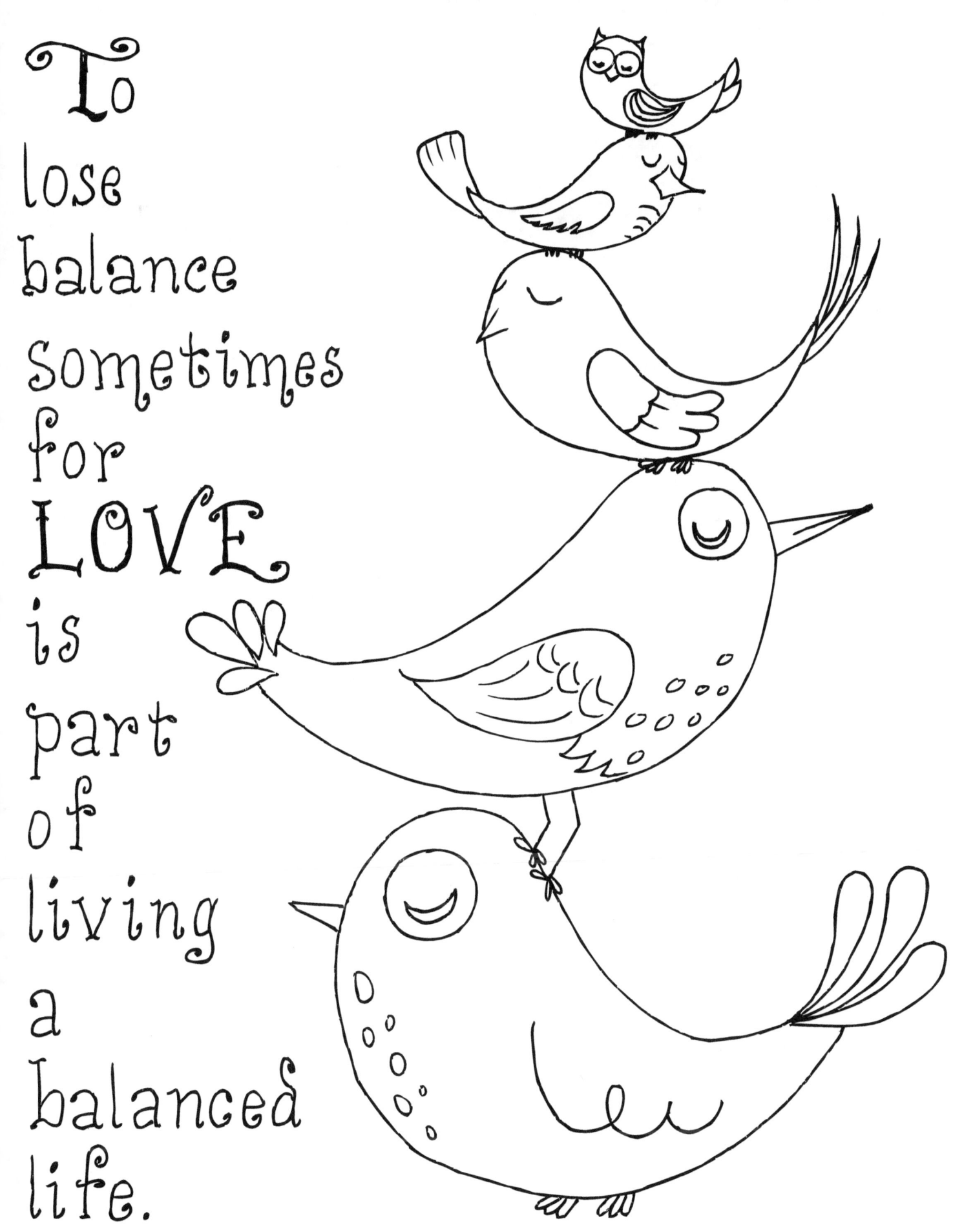

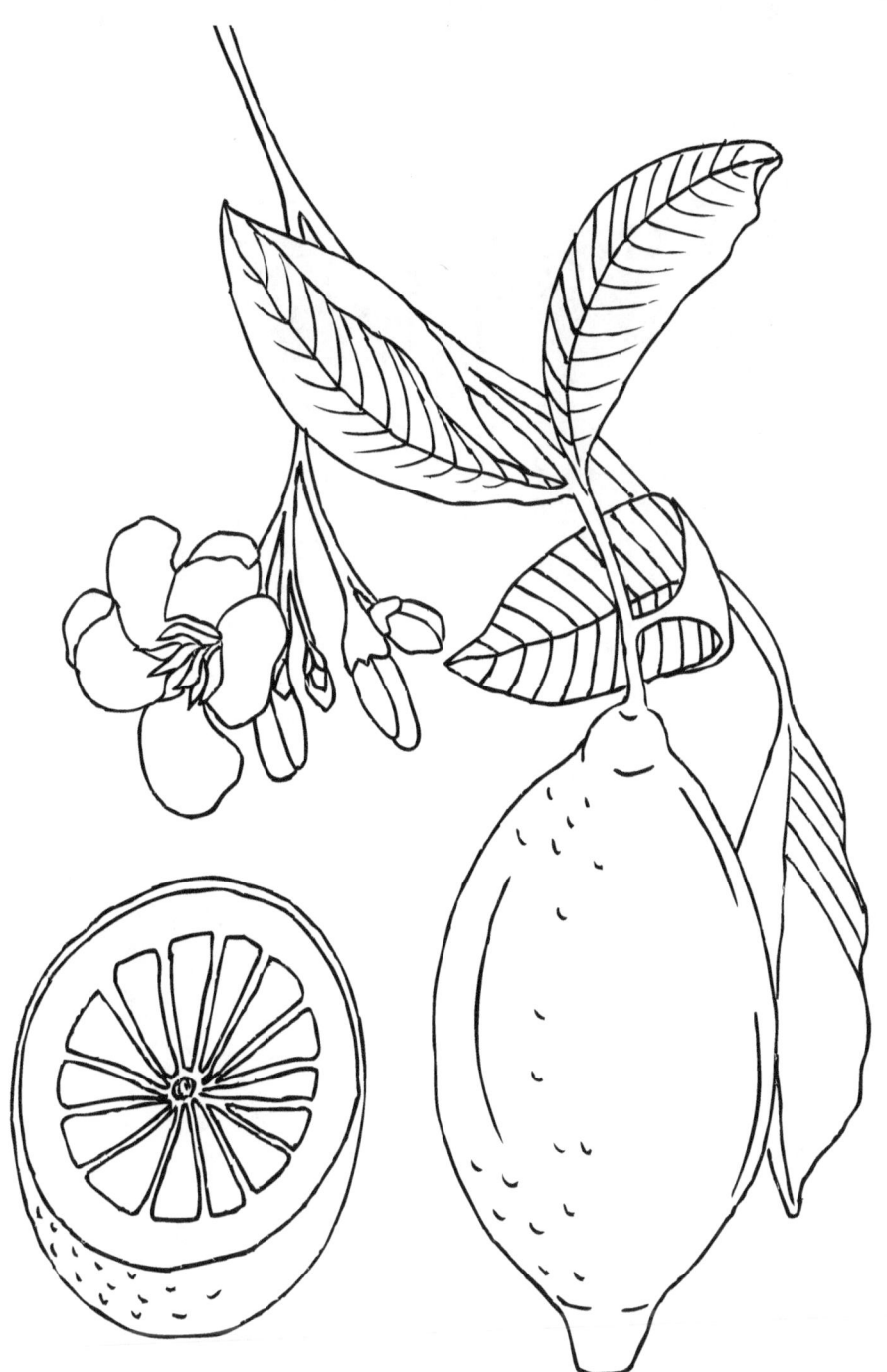

Give me the fruitful error any time, full of seeds, bursting with its own corrections. You can keep your sterile truth for yourself.

~Vilfredo Pareto

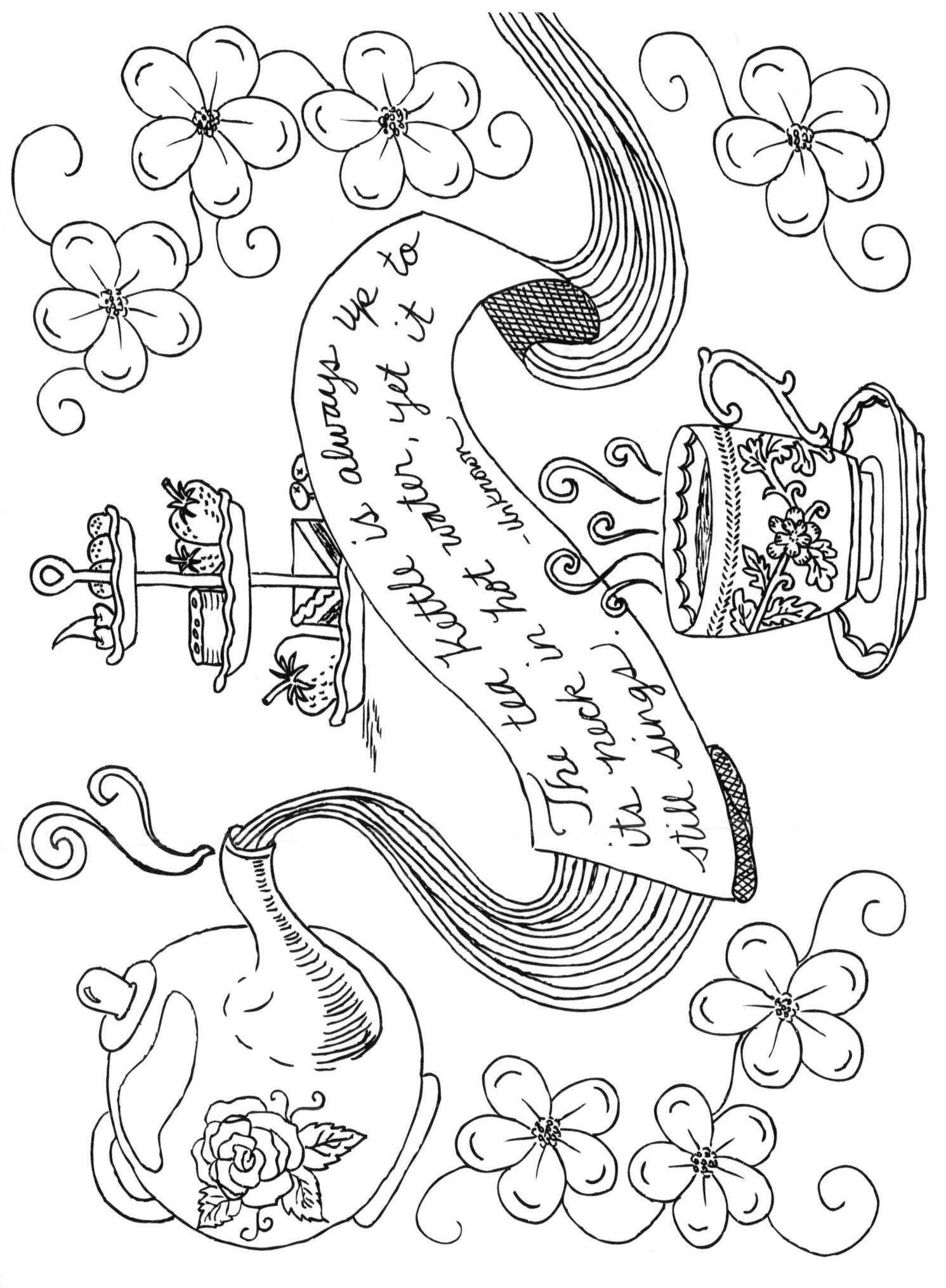

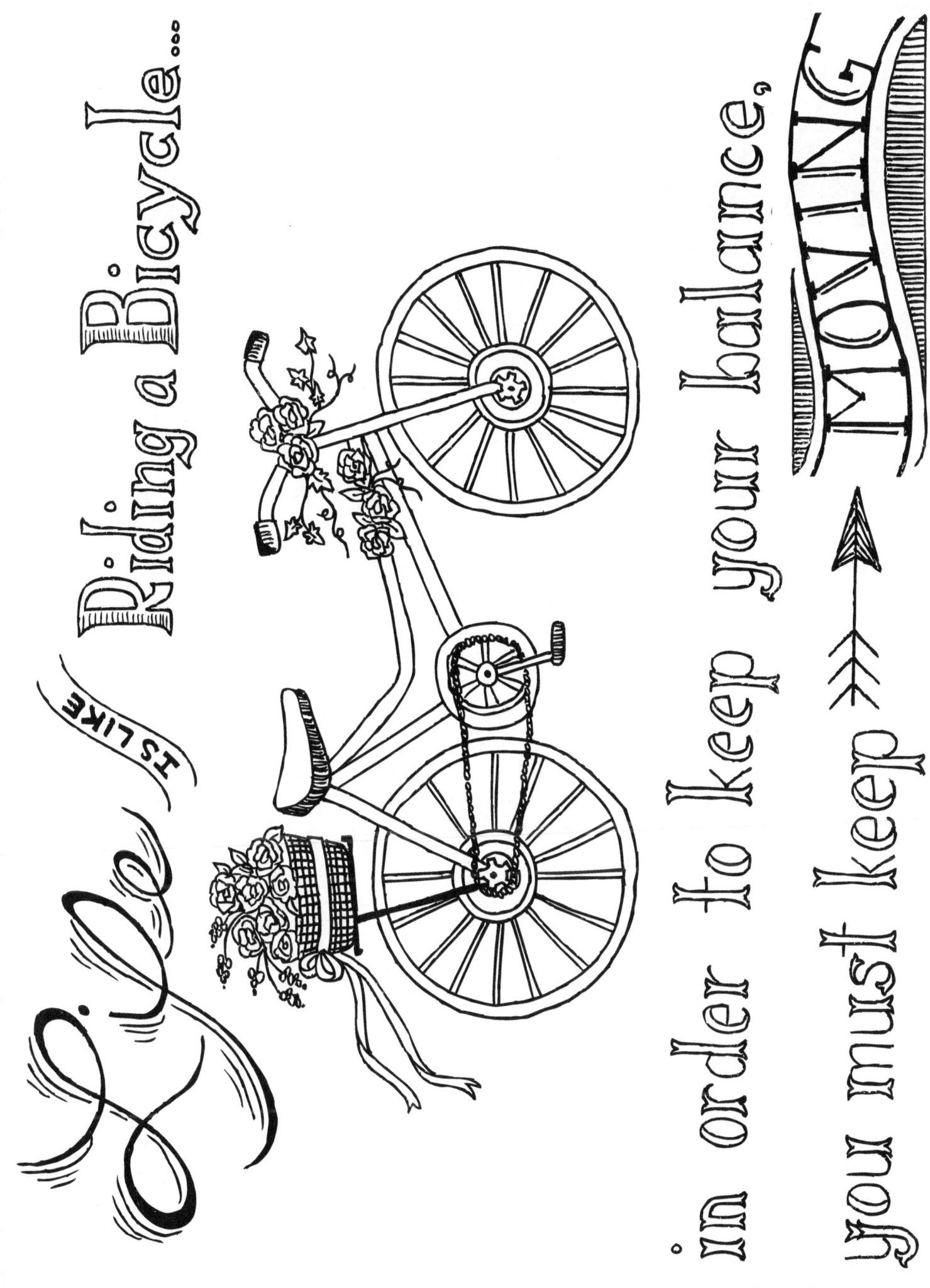

L.I.De.
IS LIKE

Riding a Bicycle...
D.I.

...in order to keep your balance,

you must keep MOVING

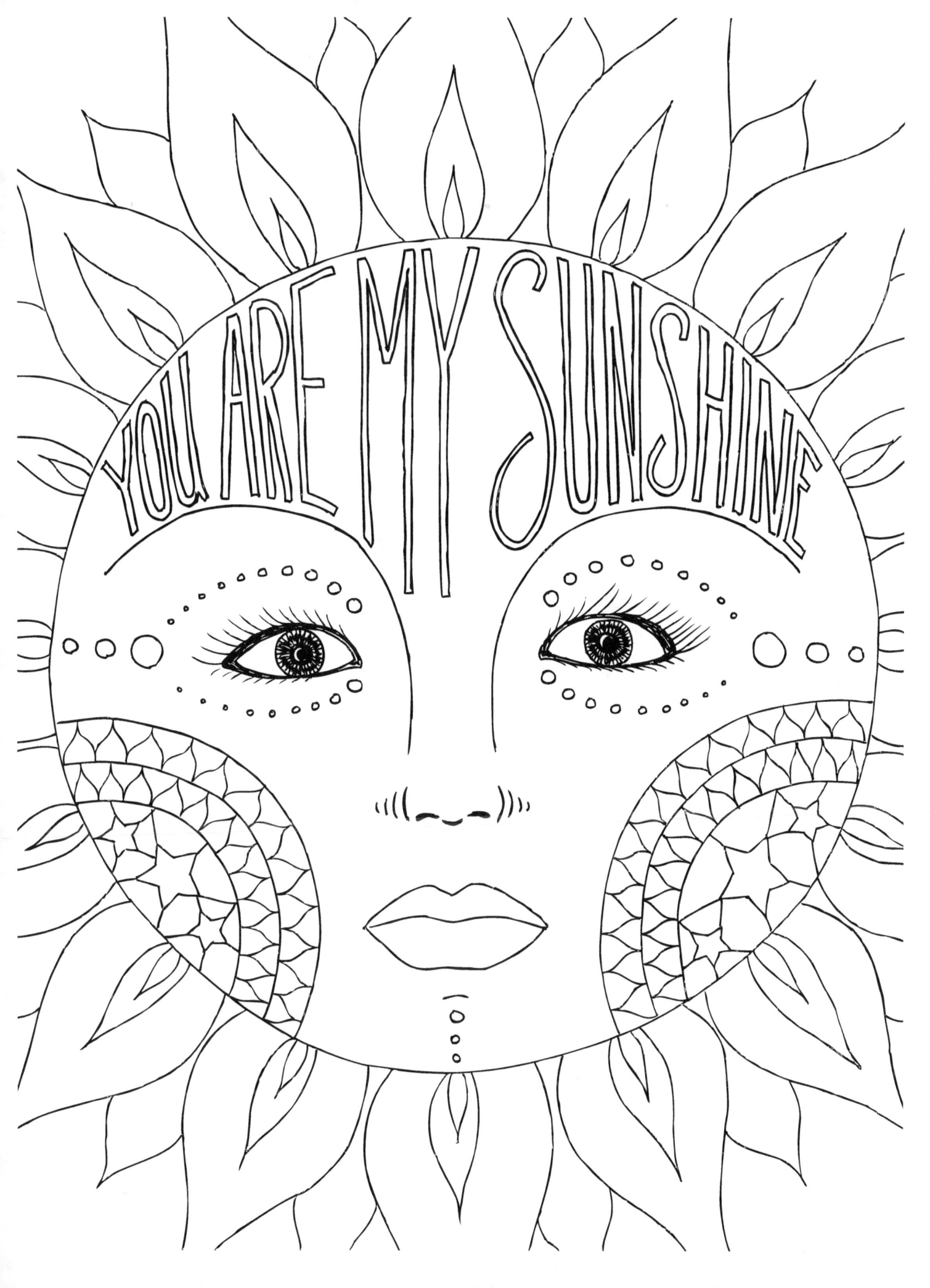

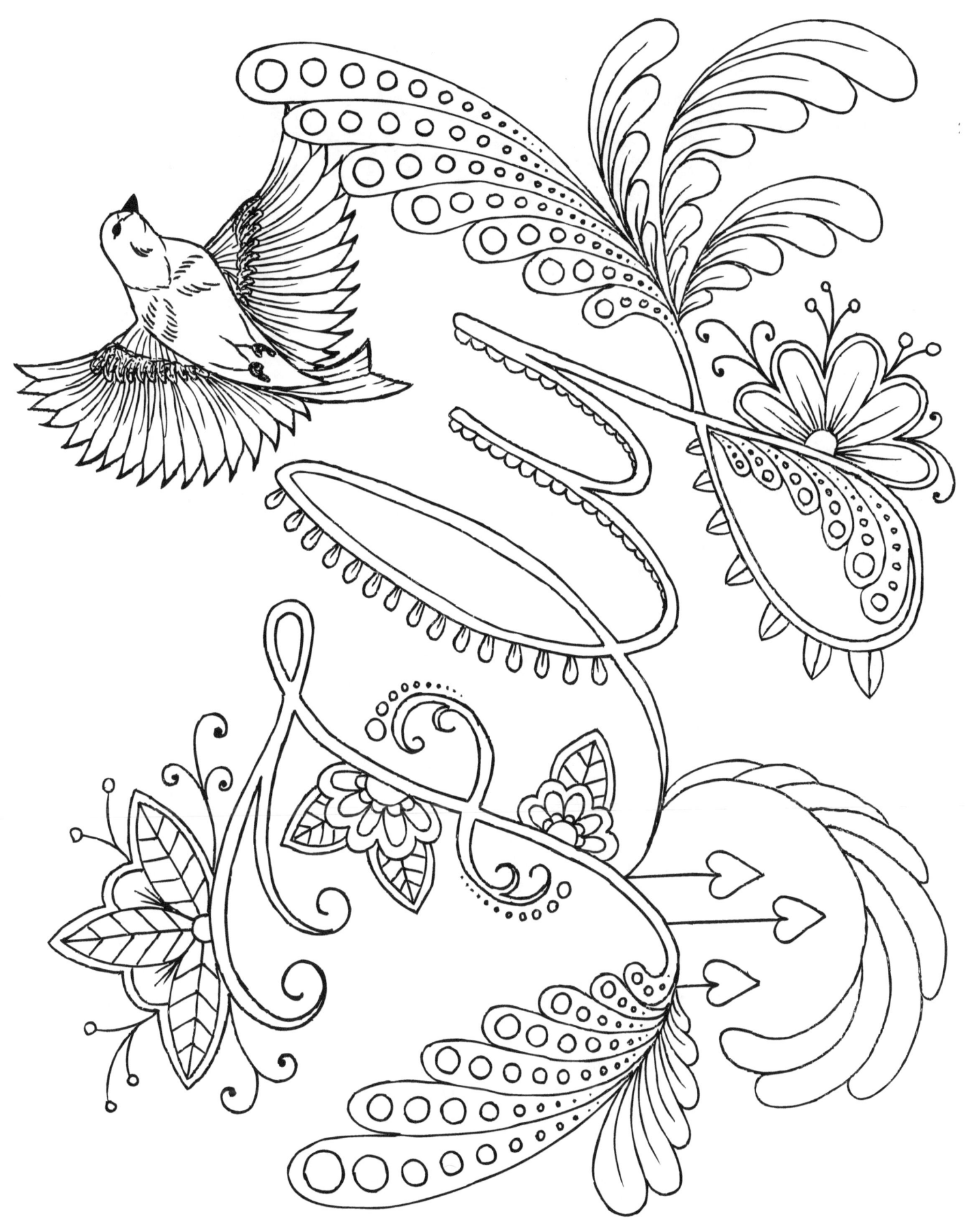

find your center

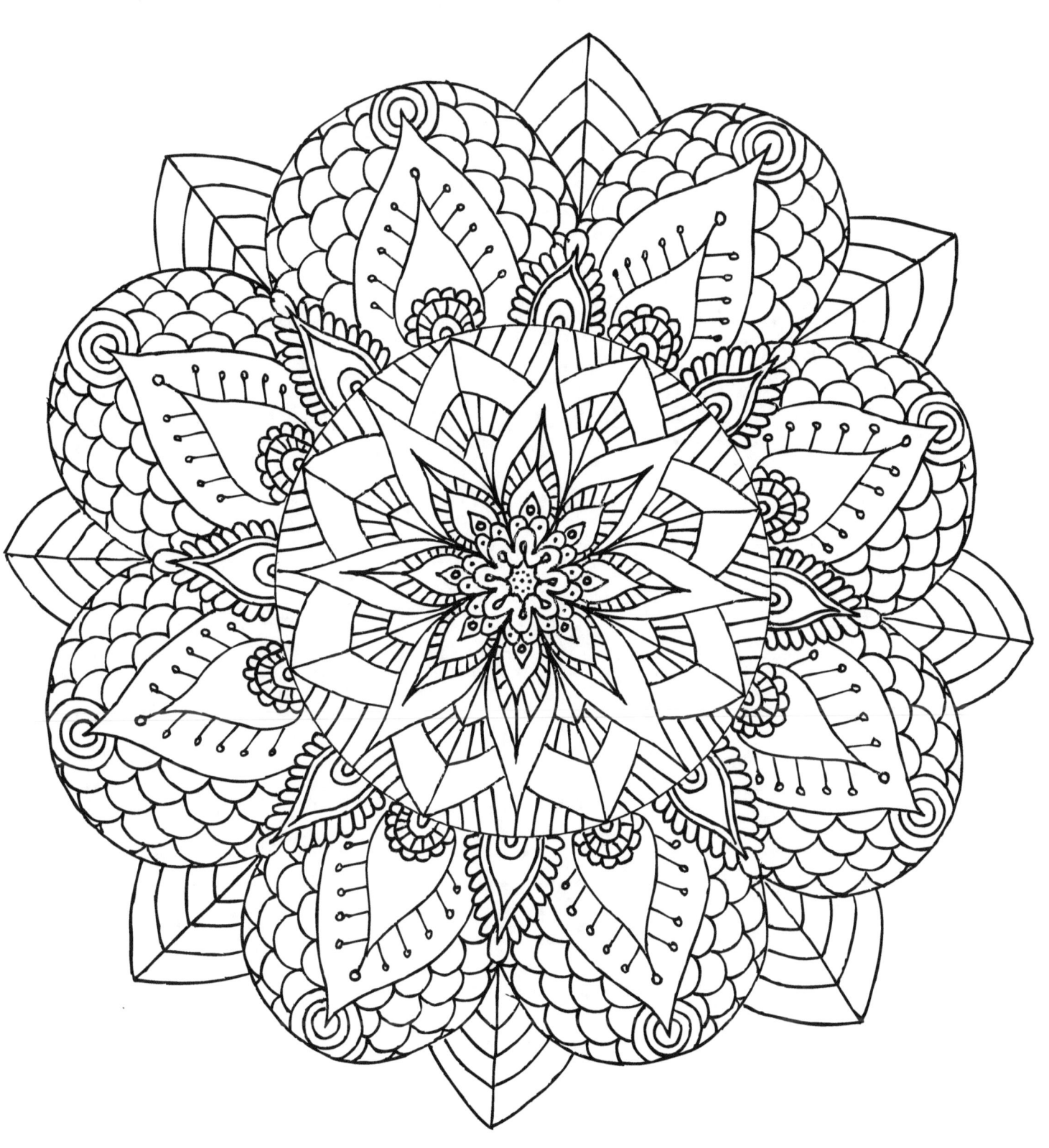

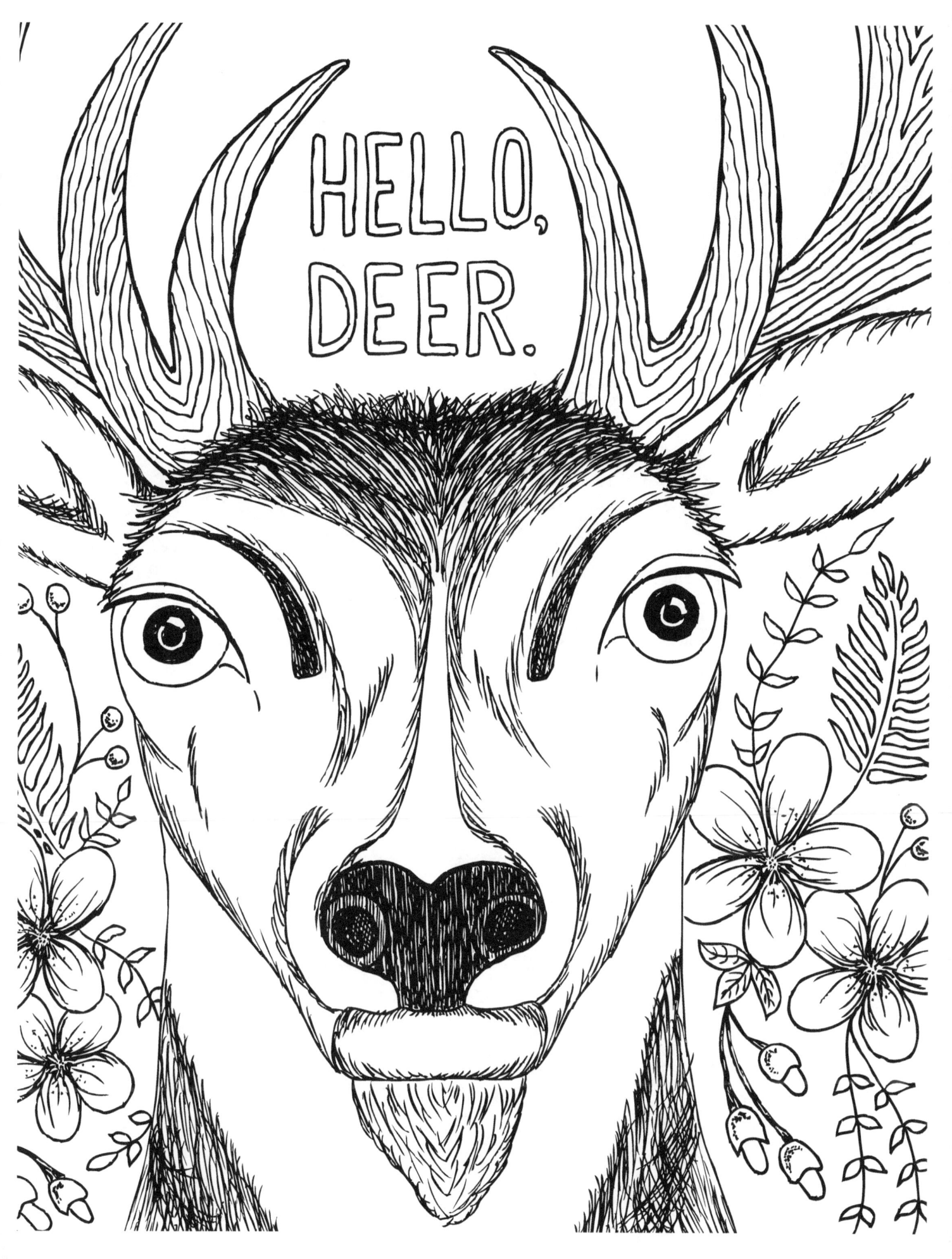

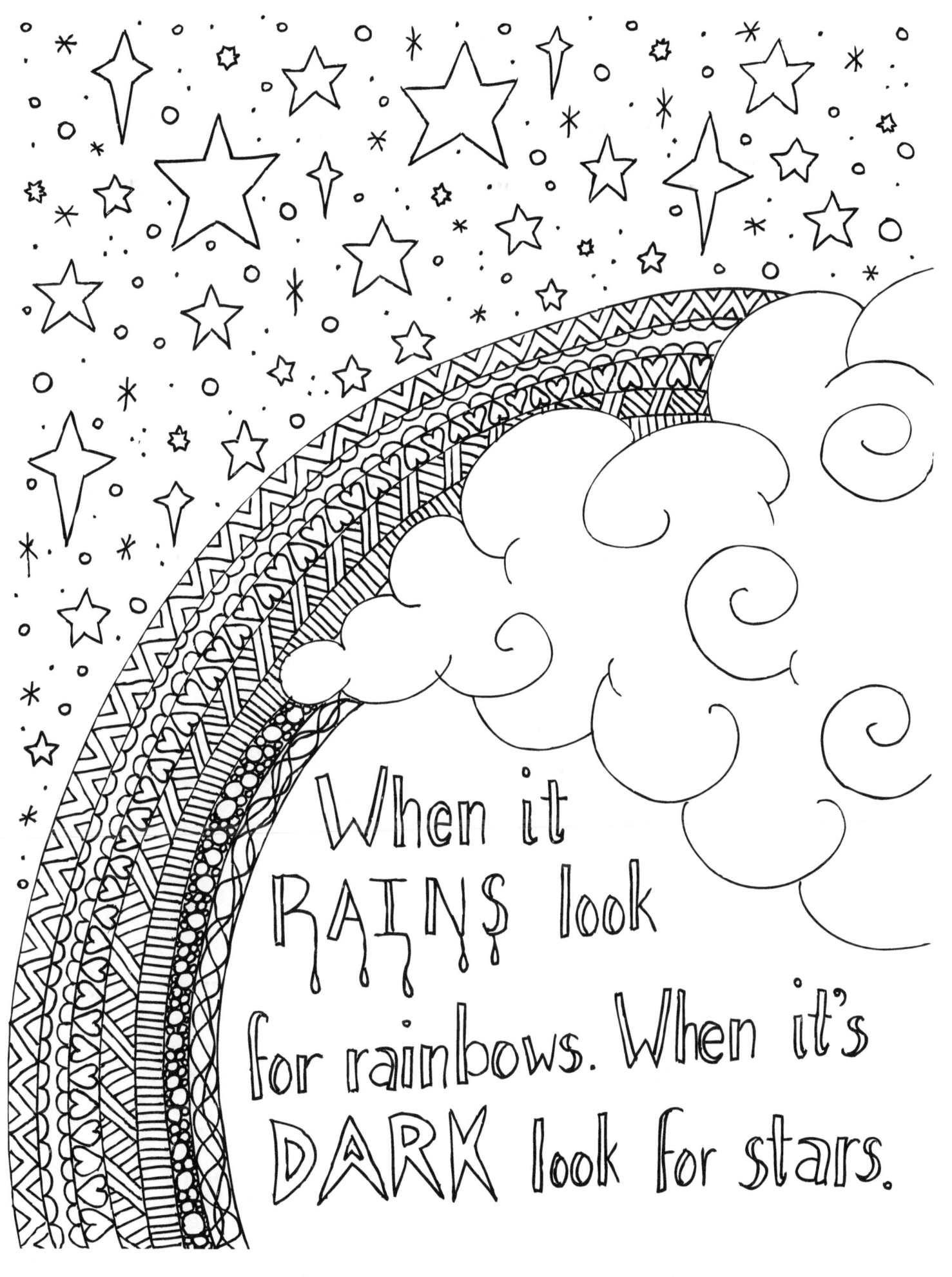

When it RAINS look for rainbows. When it's DARK look for stars.

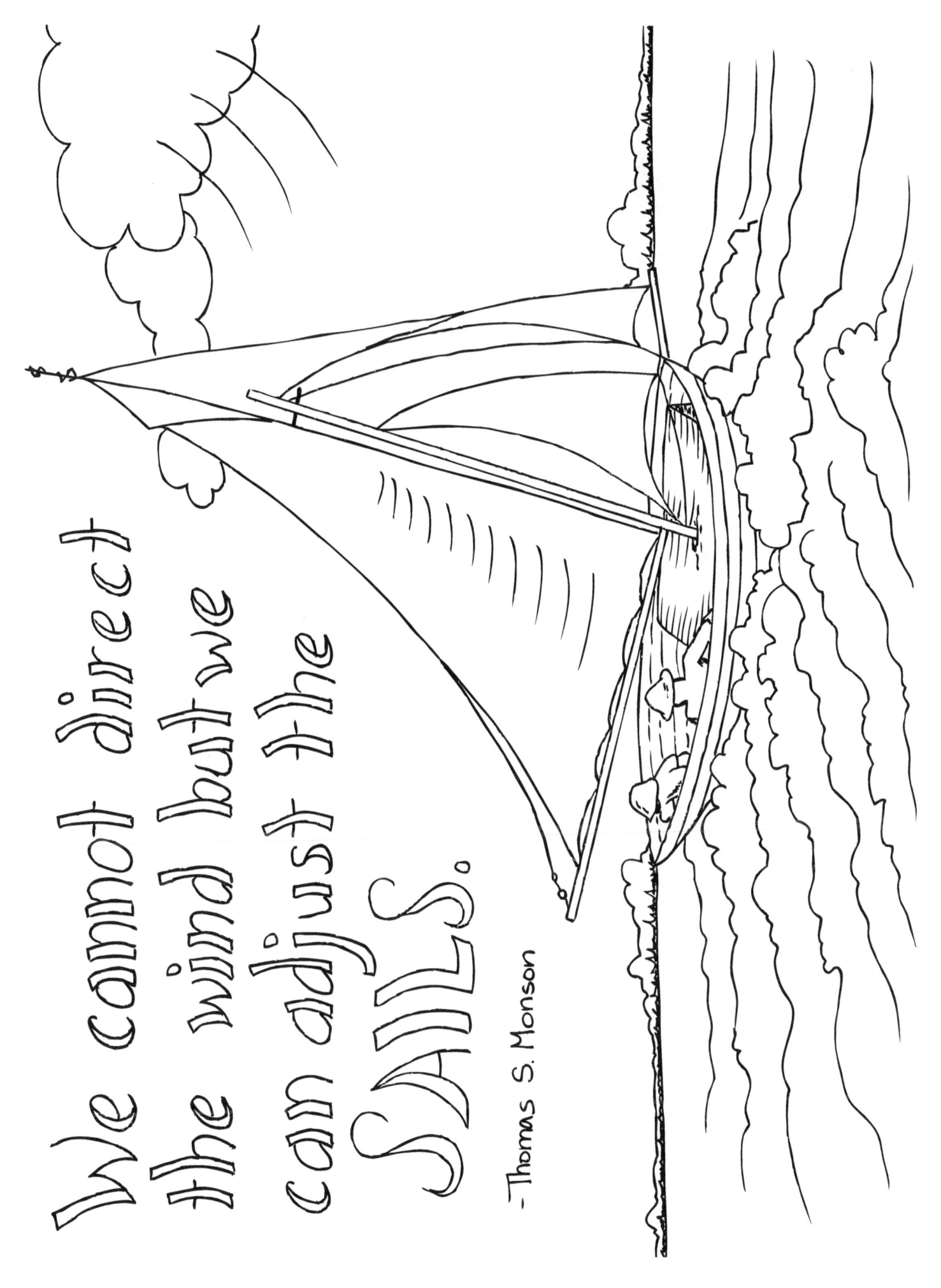

We cannot direct the wind but we can adjust the SAILS.

-Thomas S. Monson

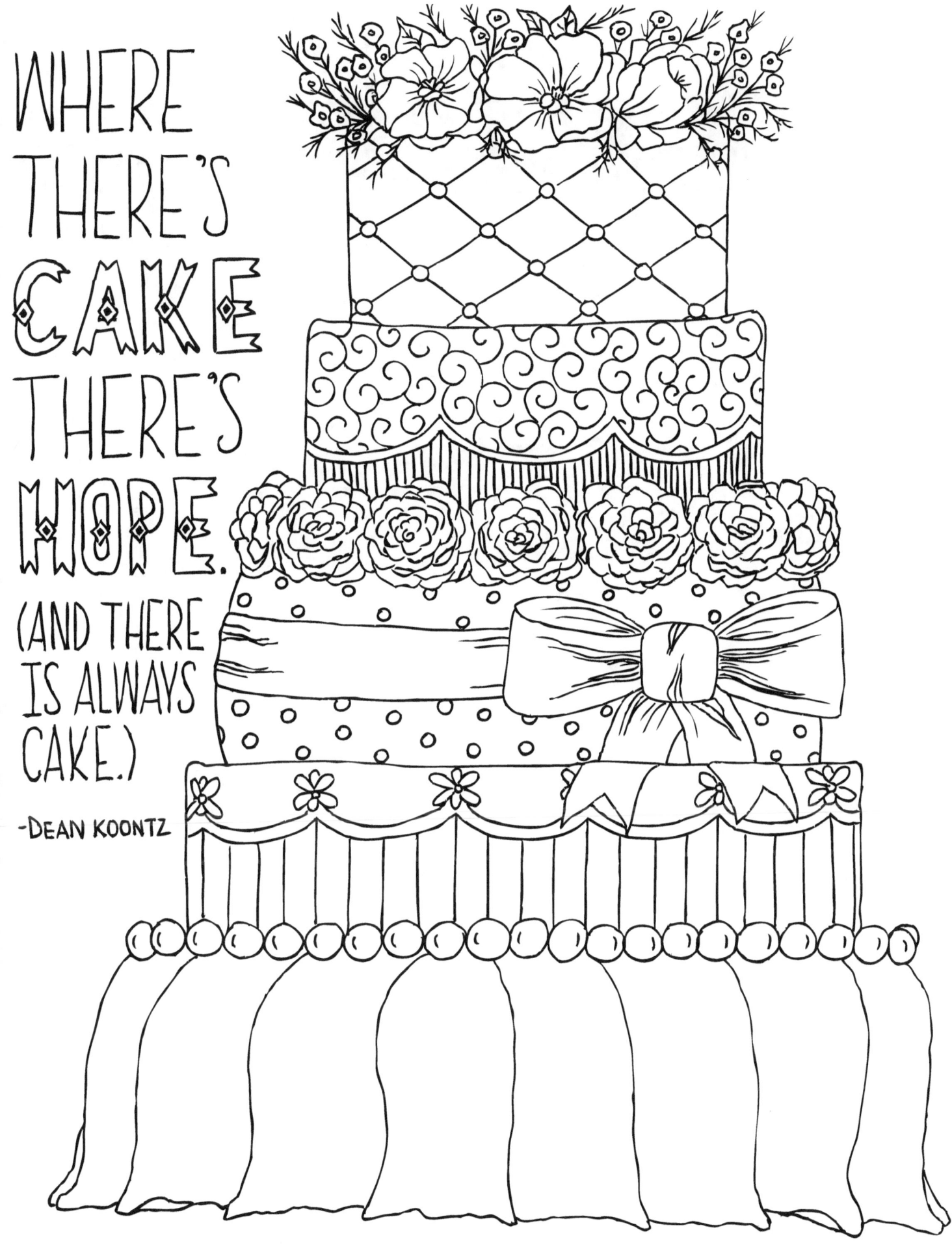

WHERE THERE'S CAKE THERE'S HOPE. (AND THERE IS ALWAYS CAKE.)

-DEAN KOONTZ

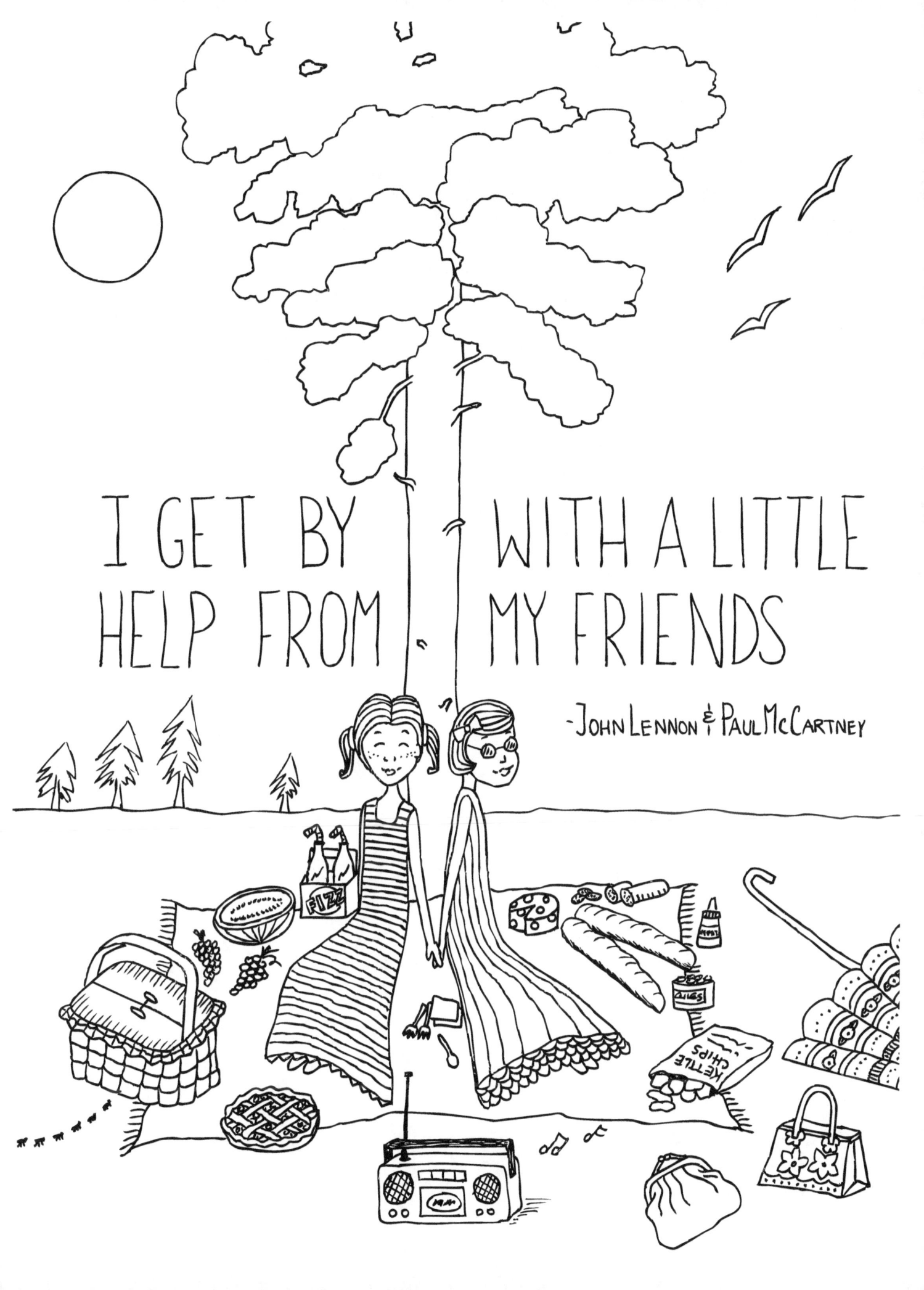

"Have I Gone Mad?"
"I'm afraid so.
You're entirely
bonkers. But
I'll tell you
a secret ...
All the best
people are."
-Lewis Carol
(Alice in Wonderland)

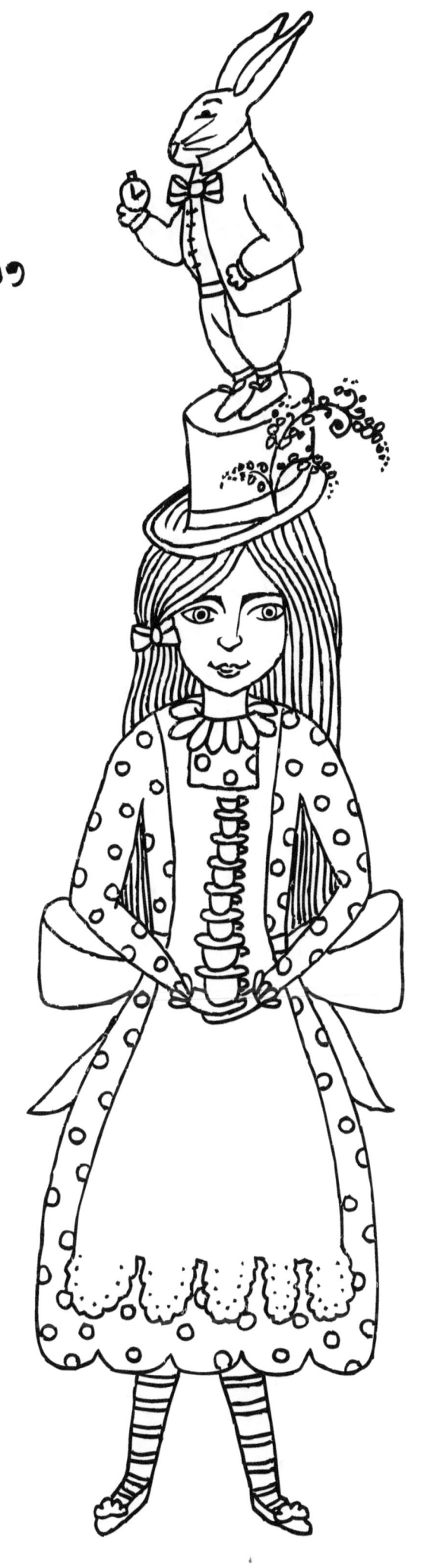

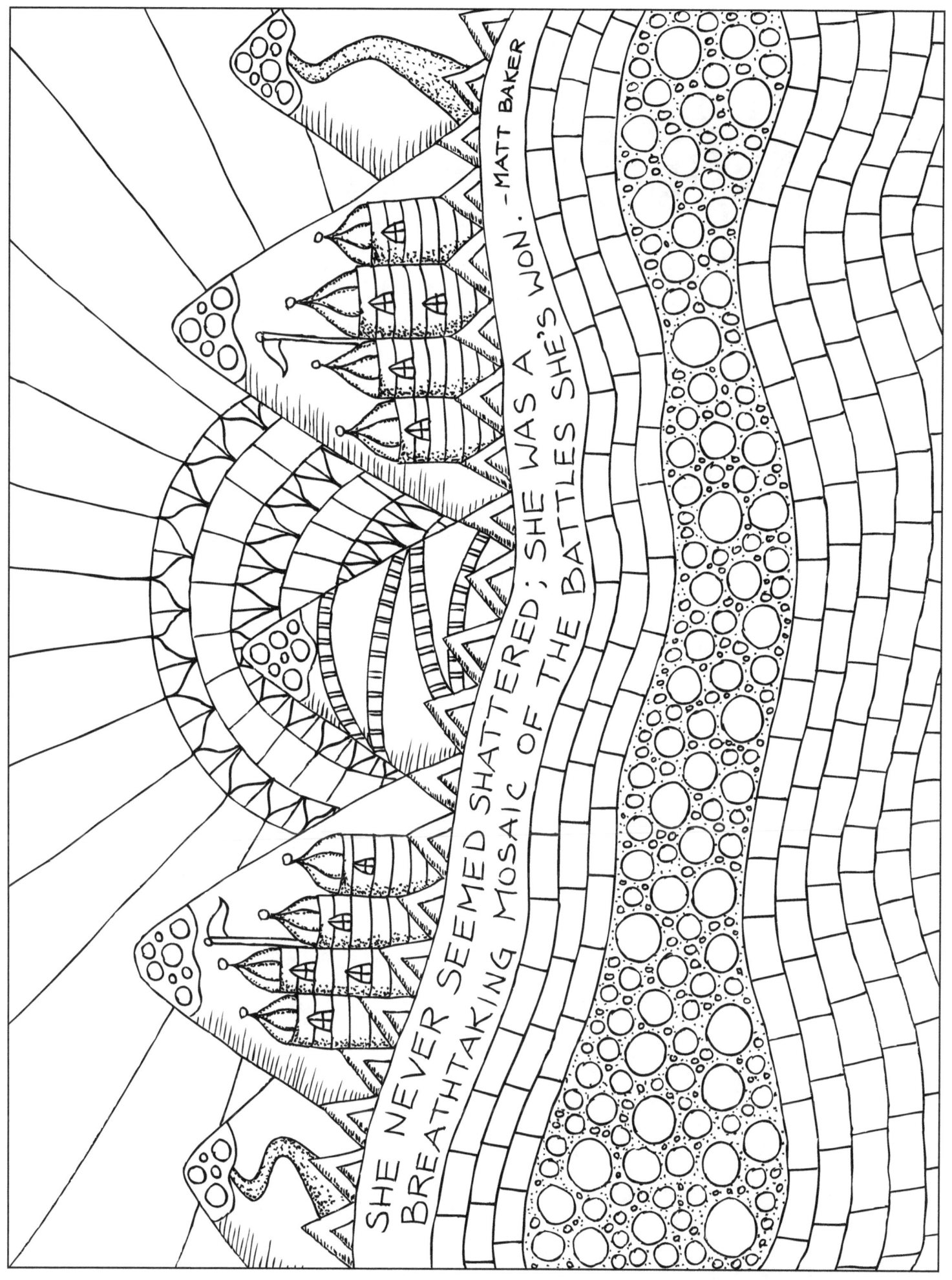

SHE NEVER SEEMED SHATTERED; SHE WAS A BREATHTAKING MOSAIC OF THE BATTLES SHE'S WON. —MATT BAKER

STAND
TALL.
WEAR A
CROWN.
BE SWEET
ON THE
INSIDE.

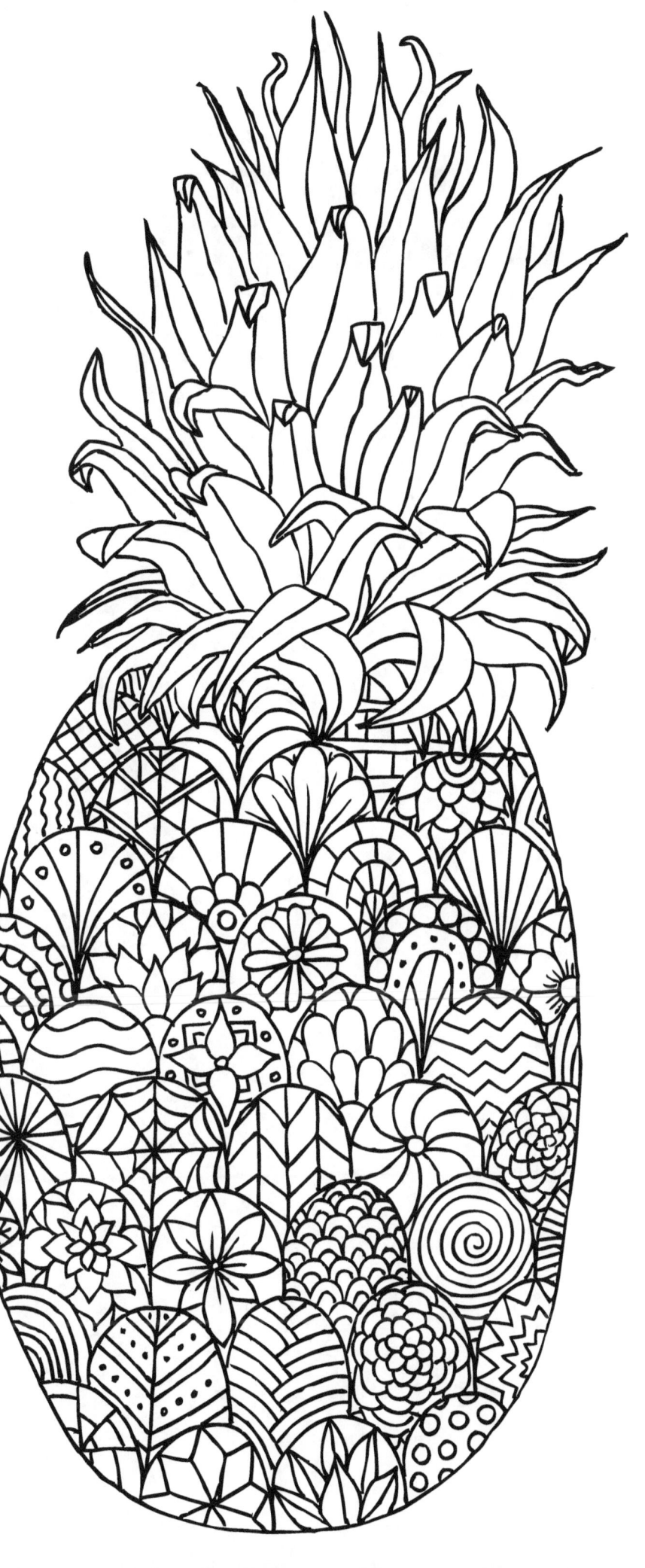

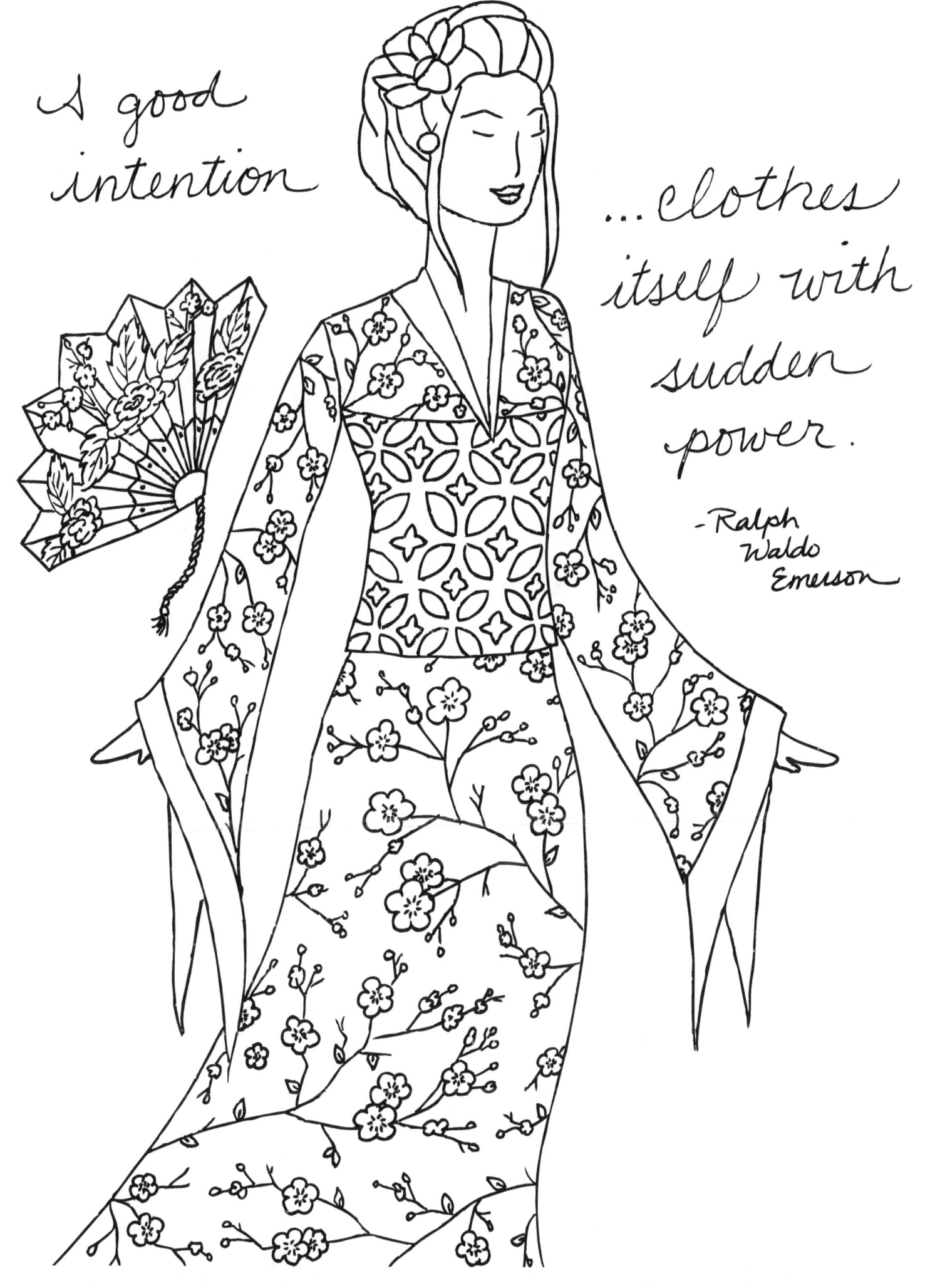

A good intention

...clothes itself with sudden power.

-Ralph Waldo Emerson

Forget not that the earth delights to feel your bare feet and the winds long to play with your hair.

-Khalil Gibran

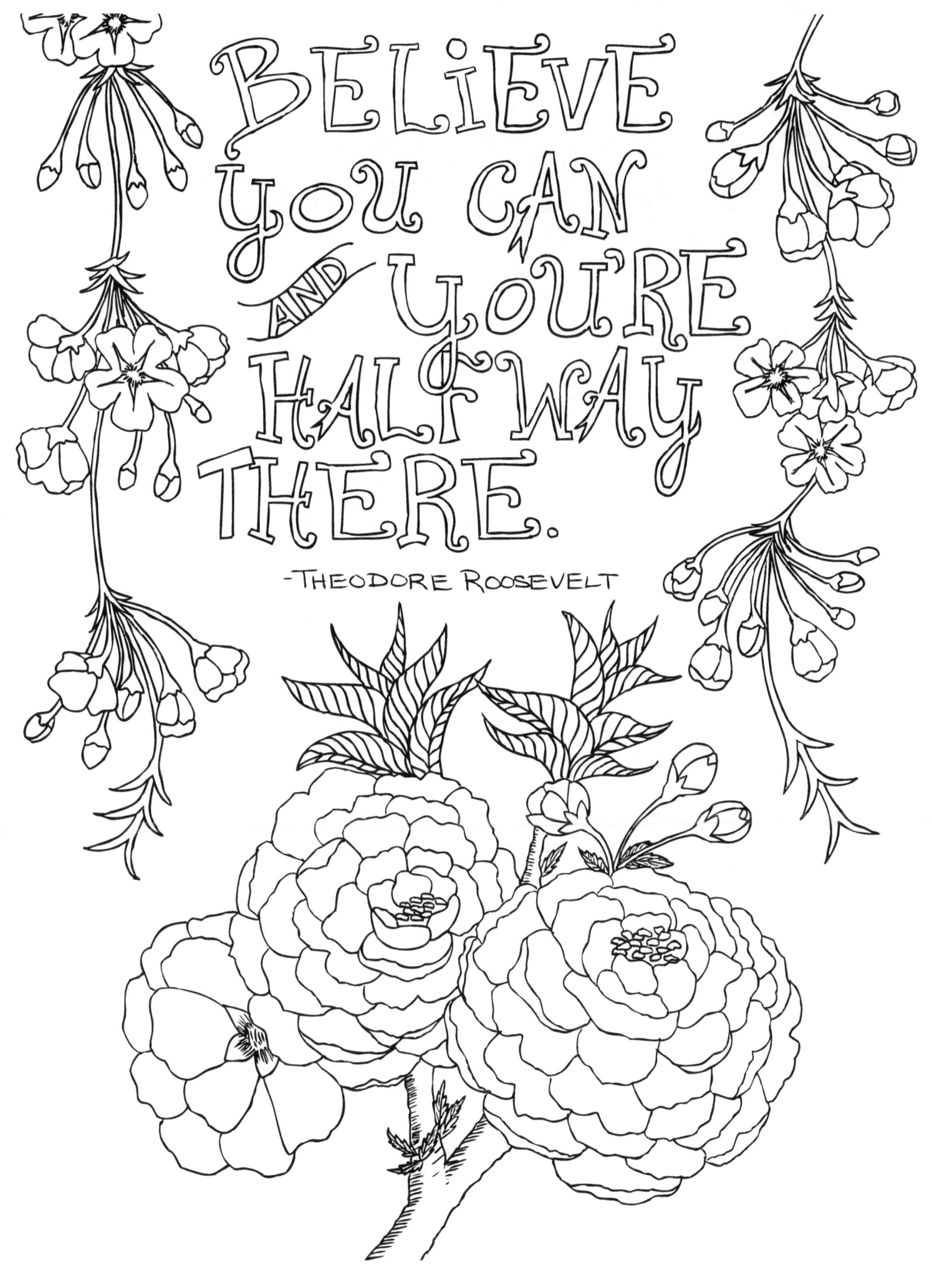

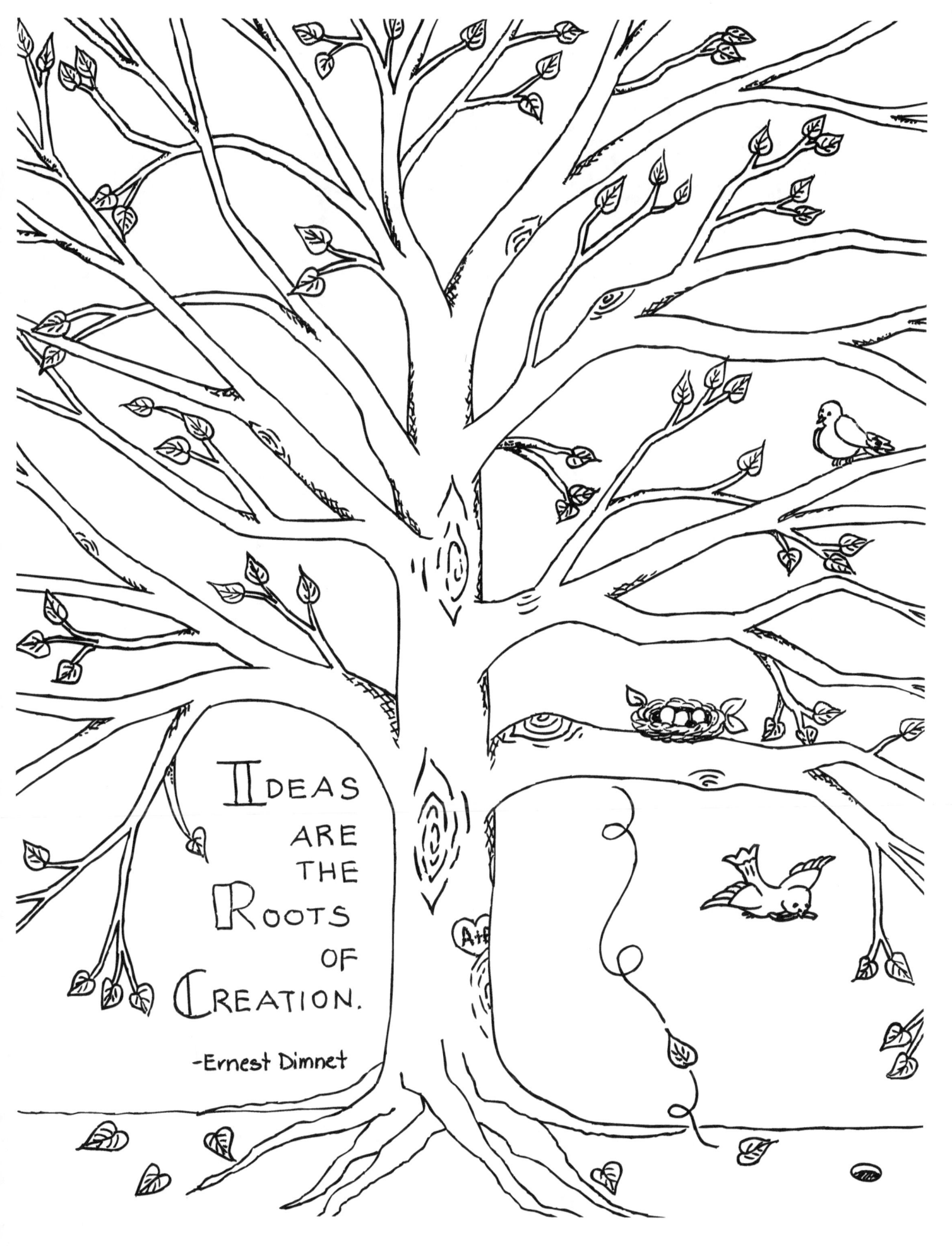

IDEAS ARE THE ROOTS OF CREATION.

-Ernest Dimnet

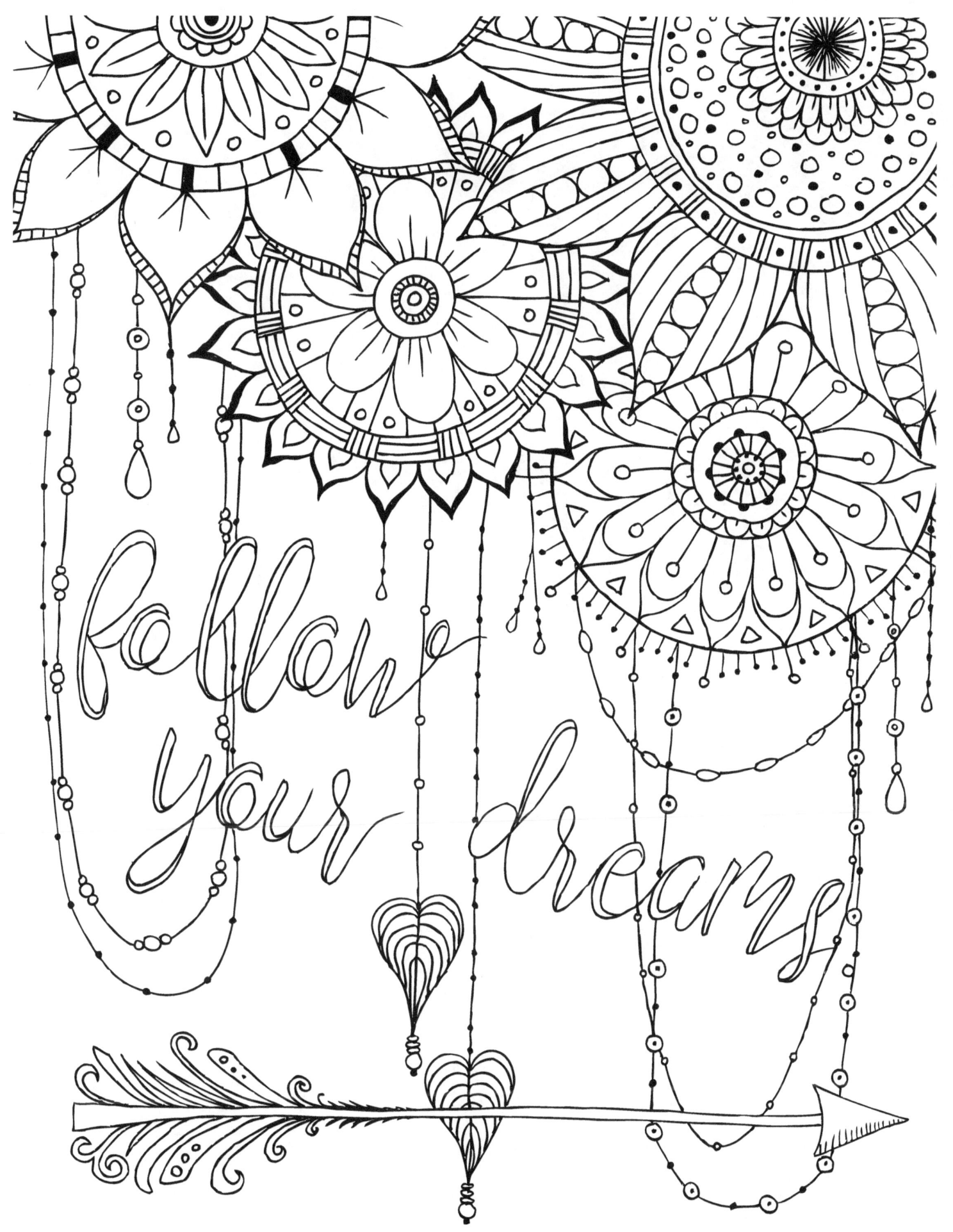

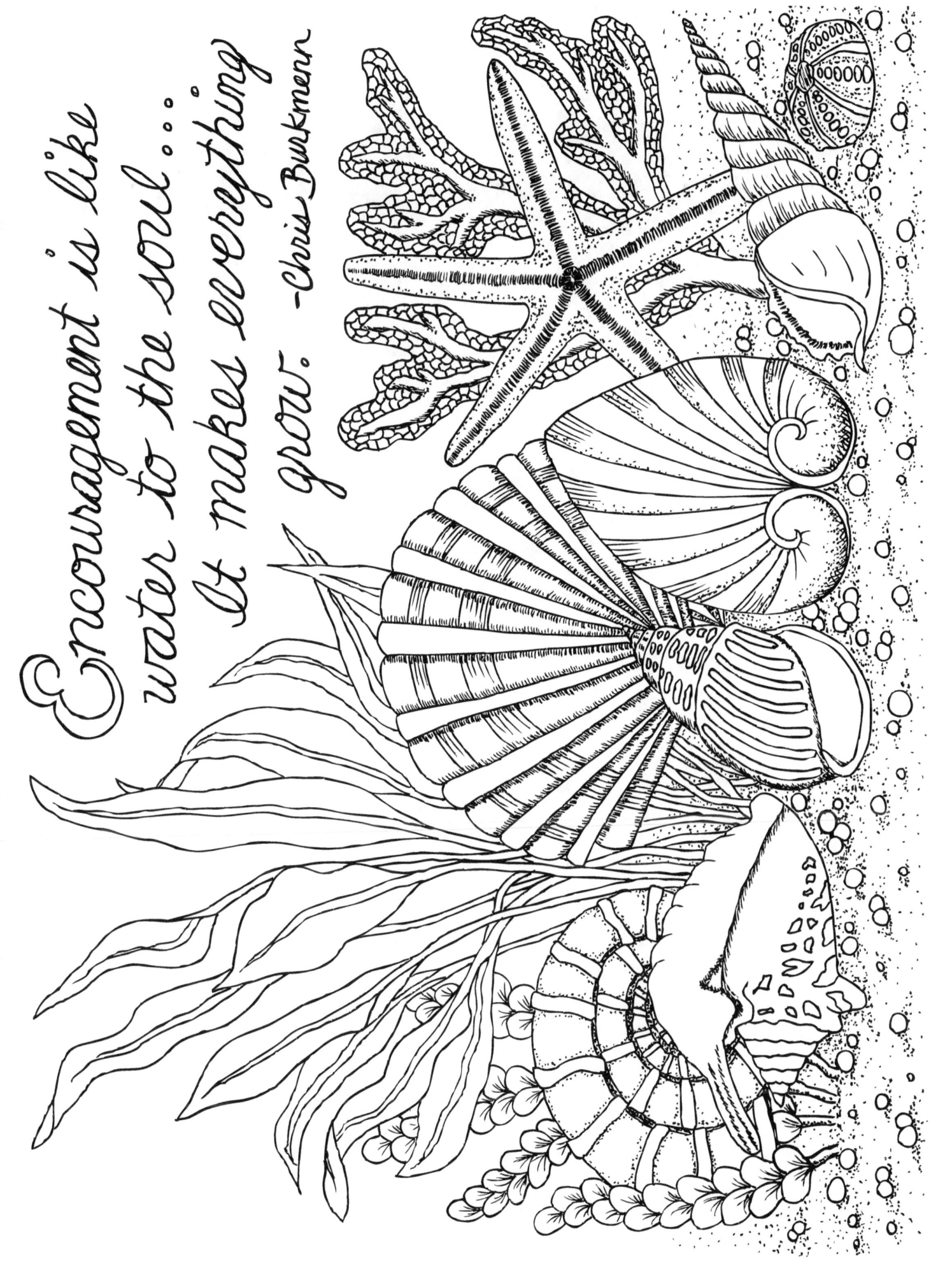

Encouragement is like water to the soul... It makes everything grow. —Chris Burkmenn

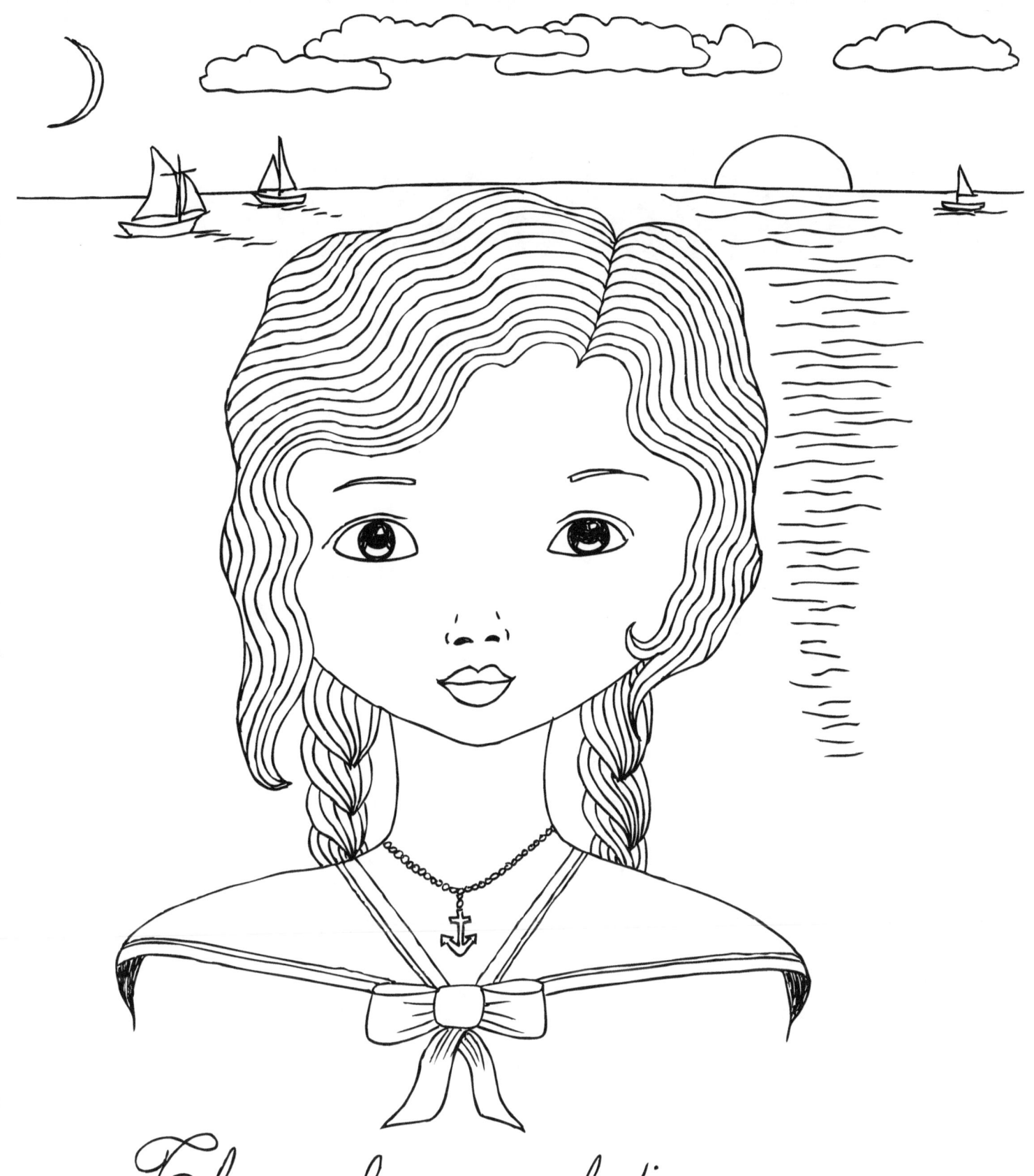

The real voyage of discovery
consists not in seeking new landscapes,
but in having new eyes.
~Marcel Proust

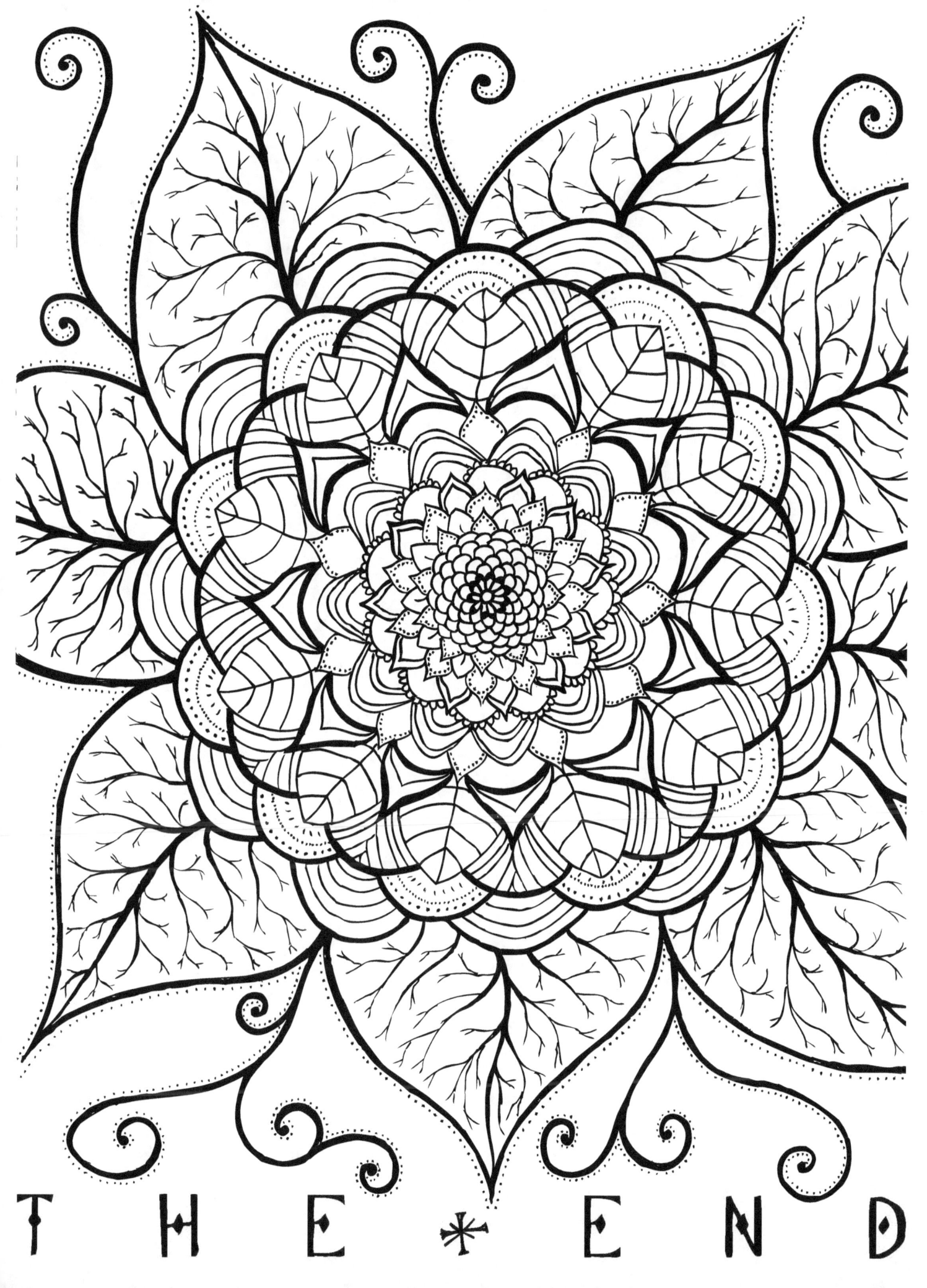

T H E * E N D

www.ingramcontent.com/pod-product-compliance
Lightning Source LLC
Chambersburg PA
CBHW080712190526
45169CB00006B/2338